MW01178205

Zen Matters
A Journey to Spiritual Triumph

Stephanie Nielson

DEDICATION

This book is dedicated to the journey. The more you trust the better the destinations you arrive at. Also to my two sons Dana and Joey. They have taught me more than I ever knew that I needed to learn and continue to be my inspiration in all that I do. Thank you, Thank you, Thank you for choosing me to be your momma, for always pushing me to be more and for filling my days with so much love.

CONTENTS

DISCLAIMER

All information in this book is provided for entertainment and informational purposes only. It is not to be perceived as professional advice in regards to health, finances or any other field. Readers who rely on the following information do so at their own risk. The author does not claim to be a professional in the area of health and wellness and it not is to be held responsible for the reader's action

"The more light you allow within you,
the brighter the world you live in will be."
~ Shakti Gawain

INTRODUCTION

It is no secret that we live in challenging times. Whether we look at our political, economic, or personal situations we are wrought with instability and chaos. The world is no longer a simple place to live and to have any semblance of success we need to keep so many balls juggling in the air that it all just seems so overwhelming at times. We hopelessly ask ourselves, "When did the responsibility of life become so unmanageable?" "What happened to the life I imagined I would have when I was a child?" "Why isn't my life like what I have seen over and over in the movies?" Days pass and we feel no relief from the crazy and the disappointment.

I am here to tell you that it does not have to be that way. Life can be fun and exciting and creative and calm and peaceful all at the same time. No matter how wrought with responsibility you may feel, you can still enjoy each moment that life has to offer you. As a matter of fact, with the right perspective, you can shift the burden of your obligations into a blessing. I am living proof that despite all the madness, one can live a happy, fulfilled and wonderful life. This is not in relation to how much responsibility you have either as trust me, I know responsibility!

I have been a single mother raising two boys since 2001. At the time of my separation my sons were 5 and 18 months old. Prior to my life as single mom, I was a stay at home mom happily devoting my life to raising my boys and taking care of my husband. My highest goal beyond keeping a clean home and learning to cook new and inspiring meals was to be part of the PTA. It was always my dream to have the quintessential family where I could devote my time and energy into supporting my husband and children. I felt that my greatest reward would be in witnessing their success.

As it usually does, life had other plans for me. For reasons, completely beyond my own control I found myself in the position of having to leave my family home. In an instant, my life had changed forever and I was completely unprepared for it. I was alone, unemployed, with no formal education and responsible for two of the most beautiful little souls you could have ever seen. It was honestly one of the most terrifying and most stressful times of my life. What was I to do? Where was I to go? How am I going to take care of my precious little children? Honestly, if it wasn't for for my maladjusted mother and the love I had for my sons I do not think I would have survived.

Being fortunate enough to live in a country like Canada, there are systems in place for people who find themselves in situations similar to mine. Assistance was available for me in order to help me get back on my feet. On that very first night away from our home (as we stayed at my mother's house), I tucked my beautiful babies into bed and looked down at their precious little faces. I understood in that moment that government assistance was not an option. I needed to do better than that for them. In my heart I knew that they deserved that I do better for them. As I watched them innocently nestle into sleep, I had such a profound understanding (the kind that could only come from source) that it was my responsibility to show my young men what it meant to work for your keep and that through hard work you can achieve anything you want.

It was deeply impressed upon me that night that I had to instill in my sons that when life gets tough you don't give up and look for handouts but you work for what you want and you find a way. And there is always a way! Although, I knew that this was a life changing moment for me, never in my wildest dreams did I ever believe that this declaration would one day have me making executive decisions while sitting in corporate boardrooms on a global level. It is funny to look back and see that my thoughts were still so limited in those days.

The next morning instead of calling social services, I called a law firm that I had just finished a two-week temporary position as a legal assistant with. Feeling exposed and vulnerable, I explained to them my situation and asked them if they had anything available full time. Although they were not looking at the moment, they were impressed with the work that I had done and had compassion for my circumstances. They started me in a part time capacity with the potential for full time as they move into their high season. I was so ecstatic, grateful, and relieved. The universe had my back long before I even had the awareness that it could! Unbeknownst to me at the time, that decision would set me on a path of independence that would change my life, my view of self and my interaction in the world and my children in powerful and remarkable ways. On a side note, the woman that hired me way back then, is still to this day a very close girlfriend of mine.

Due to my strong work ethic and ability to learn and expand at an accelerated rate, my career grew and developed exponentially. Never did I ever imagine that not only would people see my value and want me to come work for them but the fact that they were willing to pay me well for the skills that I naturally brought to the table seemed inconceivable. I was surprised how company after company would offer me advanced positions if I joined their team. That is not to say that I wasn't faced with some very challenging experiences and situations along the way, but I always rose to the occasion and thus learned so much about who I was capable to being.

As my career advanced, I started to discover my strong points and in what area I excelled. Having this understanding allowed me to be able to hone my career into a specific role in a specific industry and soon became an 'expert' at what I did. That is when everything began to soar. The money became really good and I was able to perform my duties around the schedule that I wanted. I was finally able to create some real work life balance and foster the life that I relentlessly wanted to provide for my rapidly growing boys.

I have always been a natural pupil of life so it only makes sense that I am also a natural teacher of life (It's actually in my DNA – my Grandmother was a school teacher after all). I have always had the capacity to want to share what I have learned with others. Especially when what I learn is exciting to me or when I see great benefit to its application. When I look at how far I have come in my journey and see so many others struggling I feel compelled to want to help. As a matter of fact, it feels as though it might even be my calling.

So to answer this call and to assist you with your growth, I have put together in this book what I have found to be the most important elements in my spiritual journey. I have titled this book Zen Matters for two reasons. The first, is that the art of Zen is not about belonging to a specific religion or sect and does not tell you what to believe. Zenism goes beyond Buddhism or Taoism as it simply offers one a platform to expand ones mind and consider another way of thinking. Zen Matters is exactly that. Each topic (or matter) offers the reader another way of thinking. It does not mean that you have to agree, it proposes only a consideration to expand ones perspective.

Secondly, I have titled this book Zen Matters because, well, it matters. It has been scientifically proven that our expansion of thought is a direct correlation to the level of happiness that we experience. When we are always looking for ways to grow and change we feel alive and inspired. When we stay stuck in our current state of consciousness or focus our energy on our past, we feel defeated and hopeless. As the saying goes "If we are not growing, we are dying." Once we hit the age of maturity and have completed our physical growth, the only option we then have for expansion is in our mental and spiritual development.

I know we all have it in us to live successfully. Whatever that definition is to each individual. We just need to overcome the messaging we received as children and believe in ourselves enough to carve out our own path. I wasn't born with the confidence I have today, nor the understanding of my talents either. It has been a continual process for me. To demonstrate this, I will share this interaction I recently had with my best friend. She offered me a compliment that highlighted my intelligence and how much she enjoyed the way I think. After expressing appreciation for the comment, I shared with her that due to the messaging I received growing up I didn't even know I was intelligent until I was in my mid 30ies. Up until that point, I honestly thought I was a ditz!

You see, as I reach each new step in my development my sense of self increases as does my recognition of my capabilities. Self-love and self-awareness is a journey. There is no instant fix (there is however, a shift in perspective and happiness that can be obtained quite easily). I continuously practice each step that I offer in this book and am constantly in awe with what I learn about myself, about others and about life. These steps have helped me build a super strong foundation so that no matter what storms pass by, I always remain strong and grounded. So with no further ado, I invite you to open your mind, open your heart and discover what expansion of thought can take you to your next level of life.

Let's begin shall we…

"Upon wakening let the words thank you flow from you lips, for this will remind you to begin your day with gratitude and compassion."
~Dr. Wayne Dyer

Chapter 1

THE GREATNESS OF GRATITUDE
Step 1

The Concept:

For me, finding gratitude has been one of the simplest yet most powerfully transforming practices in my spiritual development. Learning to be grateful for all of my experiences, good or bad, has been one of the greatest blessings I have ever received. The empowerment that I experienced from understanding this modest practice has been immense! From gratitude I've gained humility, happiness, peacefulness and hope. It has also been the starting point for my self-love, my love of others, my vulnerability, in finding forgiveness, in being present and it has most definitely changed my overall perspective. Gratitude is the most powerful and significant of our secondary emotions. For gratitude begets love and in the end, love is all it is ever about.

The benefits of living a life in gratitude are endless. Research has shown that when we start to regularly practice gratitude we begin to experience more positive emotions, feel more alive, sleep better, express more compassion and kindness, and even have stronger immune systems. I can attest to all of that! The more we find to be grateful for, the more of these incredible benefits we receive. It is important to remember that gratitude doesn't need to be reserved for the large occasions in our lives such as a job promotion or the purchase of a new home. We can find gratitude in things as simple as a recipe turning out well or getting inspired at just the right moment. Continuously reflecting on and rejoicing in the moments for which we're thankful will significantly increase our well-being and satisfaction of life.

I realize that it isn't easy to have gratitude when things feel like they are falling down around us. How can we focus on the good when everything feels so bad? When we are experiencing trying times, finding gratitude not only keeps our spirits from taking a dive but it also allows for us to bring a different perspective to the table and find solutions that we may otherwise miss. Bringing gratitude to our challenges helps us to find quicker, clearer answers because we're not in a panic about the current situation. Living in gratitude won't free our lives of problems, but it will make them feel much less daunting and reduce their frequency.

If you consider the perspective that what we focus on expands we can clearly see how gratitude during difficult times can be beneficial. To demonstrate this point I will share with you a little personal story. It was during another period of transition in my life. I was working for a company that I had been with for a few years and had received a significant transfer request the year before. After a year of working in my new territory it became clear how unsatisfied I was with the arrangement. I was frustrated with the lack of authority I was given and did not see eye to eye with my new manager on how he went to market. The worst part was that during the week my position kept me away from my family home where my teenage son was left to fend for himself. My feelings of unhappiness were growing and growing to the point that I would feel anxiety in my belly on a regular basis.

Although the situation was becoming increasingly gloomy, I conscientiously committed to continue to find all the things that I was grateful for. I was even grateful for the negative feelings I was experiencing as I recognized that they were providing clarity on what I did not want. Each day I would thank Source for the opportunity to recognize what it was that I desired and for bringing forth an opportunity that would better suit my lifestyle. I reached out to people that may be able to help me find another opportunity and even responded to a headhunter that had reached out to me a while back. Before I knew it I was embarking upon a new path in a position that not only took me to the next level of my career but also increased my salary exponentially. The best part however, was that I would be able to be at home with my son each night. I truly believe that it was due to my attitude of gratitude during this stressful time that I was able to move forward in such a positive direction.

Gratitude will also increase the quality of our relationships. Let's be honest. No one wants to spend their time with Debbie Downer or Cathy Complainer. I sure don't. When we bring a positive, grateful attitude to life, people are drawn to us. We see it with strangers and acquaintances, and the relationships we have with the people we are closest to begin to shift as well. When we show appreciation to those we care about they become more responsive to our needs and their commitment increases. When we live in appreciation we tend to do more for one another and become much more satisfied with our relationships. Although research has shown that just the feeling of gratitude for our people will increase the level of satisfaction in our relationships, expression of that appreciation will bring it to the next level. We should embrace the act of expressing gratitude to our loved ones when they do something for us, no matter how big or how small. This is where our relationships will truly expand.

The most wonderful effect of gratitude is that with continuous practice our lives will increase exponentially in abundance and happiness. During wonderful times or during difficult times, we can always find something to be grateful for. Yes, of course it's easy during the good times, but no matter how difficult things may seem, there is always something that we can find to appreciate, even if it is just going to sleep so we can wake to a new day tomorrow. As the saying goes, "every cloud has its silver lining." Now here is the wonderful irony of gratitude: the more often we are able to find gratitude within our world, the more we attract that for which to be grateful. Experience leaves me no choice but to suggest that gratitude is the first focus for those wishing to change any situation in their life.

My History:

I would like to share with you a little story regarding an epiphany I had while writing this book that relates to gratitude. I was having lunch with my amazing niece Hailey Bailey who is just beginning her journey as an adult in this beautiful world that we live in. I was feeling honored to impart on her some of the wisdoms that I have learned during my own journey. You see, when I have an opportunity to share my learning with anyone I feel as though I am sincerely walking in my truest calling. When that sharing is with someone who is at the start of their story (especially when that person is someone I hold so close to my heart) I feel absolutely elated and full of purpose.

The cool thing is, the more elated I feel, the more connected to source I become. The more connected to source I become, the more elated I feel and the messages just start to flow! So here I was happily telling my gorgeous niece my story, offering her insights that she could bring into her own journey and joyously engaging in every moment we were connecting together. Suddenly I realized the source of my sever writer's block in creating this book.

Yes, it's true! I was stuck and had been for months! This did not make any sense to me as I had my outline all done and knew exactly the message that I wanted to share. I had logically arranged all the chapters, put together my format and had even created an overview for each step. This book should have just written itself. Yet here I was on chapter four, standing in front of a very large wall! What made even less sense was that I was about to write about gratitude. Anyone who knows me knows that gratitude is the basis of all that I am and all that I believe in! Thereby it was only logical that it should be the easiest chapter for me to write. I had gratitude down pat. So what was the issue?

As I shared my learning with my gorgeous girl, I was telling her how the first and most important thing we all need is self-love. Makes sense, no? I went on to explain that when we truly love who we are, our inner world and our outer world will become congruent and great things begin to happen. She shared with me her recent journey of self-discovery and asked me how I came to love myself and be as confident as I am today. As much as I tried to focus on self-love (to correspond with the steps in my book of course) no matter what I told her, it all came back to gratitude. It became clear to me in that conversation that it was gratitude that truly revolutionized my spiritual journey and it was gratitude that offered me the grace to fall in love with myself. How can I begin my book with self-love when in reality it was gratitude that made me take my first step into the life I live today?

Coming to this realization not only freed me from my writers block but it also taught me three very valuable lessons that I want to share with you before we begin our journey together:

The first lesson; no matter how far you have come on your spiritual journey there is always so much more for you to learn. Stay open! These lessons can come just as much from someone who is early in their spiritual development as it can from someone who is so far ahead of you that you think you could never catch up. Never discriminate and never think that you are above or below anyone. We are all here to learn together and grow with one another.

The second lesson; when sharing your spiritual journey you need to stay in 'your' truth. Don't get so caught up in what you think people want to hear or on the format or on how you think something should go. Trust in yourself and let Source be your guide. The more you let go and just go with the flow the more things will fall into the place they need to be.

Last but not least, the third lesson; you will learn what you need to learn in the order that you need to learn it. We are all unique beings. Our awareness and our stories will put us in perfect alignment each and every time. This I can promise! The steps in this book are offered to you as a guideline based on MY experience. They may or may not resonate with you in the order in which I have written them or in the context that I have expressed them. And that is perfectly ok by the way! The goal is to get you thinking. If you stay out of your head and listen with your heart, you will always be inspired to learn what you need to learn where and when you are ready to learn it. So let's get back to gratitude and how it transformed my life shall we.

In 2009 while the economy was still reeling from the 2008 economic crash, I, like many, was on the brink of losing everything. My ego and I had worked so hard to prove to everyone (including myself) that I was no longer the impetuous blonde girl who always found herself in trouble and that I was indeed capable of looking after myself and my children. Yet here I was, unemployed, alone and without any advanced education feeling like I was once again proving all the naysayers right. I was ashamed, I was scared and I did not know what to do. No one was hiring and my options looked bleaker and bleaker by the day.

My sister offered me an opportunity to work with her in her design studio doing odd jobs and such a couple days a week with the option of learning about interior design. I had always been a natural creative and held a strong interest in all things architecture and design so I was intrigued by the offer. Not to mention, I could surely use the $15/hr as there was nothing else coming in and every little bit helped. My sister lived 45 minutes away and it was hardly worth the journey but the income was better than nothing and it did allow for me to spend some time with her. It was also during the summer and she and her husband had a beautiful yard so it was nice for my kids as well. The gifts were all there, but I was hardly in the right mindset to recognize them.

Truth be told, I was angry and resentful that I found myself in this situation. I could not understand how after all that I had been through and how hard I had worked that God would take it all away from me. My ego and I were so disillusioned. We could not understand how we could have fallen so far from grace. Until the day when I found myself in a growing rage of anger while ironing sheets for a show room. All the while chatting away with my ego about how I did not deserve to be in this situation. How below me it was. That I deserved so much more than a meagerly $15/hr. My ego and I were really on a roll!

Suddenly I heard a voice as clearly as if someone was standing next to me say "Why can you not see the gifts that are being given to you? Do you know how many people would love to have the opportunity that you are being given right now? What makes you think that you are not exactly where you need to be?"

These questions resonated with me so deeply that they brought me to tears. I realized in that moment that spirit was right! I was looking at my situation from a completely skewed perspective. Everything happens as it should and even the darkest of times can bear gifts that can alter the trajectory of our lives. This was certainly the case for me.

When I finished ironing and making the bed I went to find my sister. I shared with her my revelation and we laughed and cried and shared together. She told me that the reason she wanted to help me out so much was that her and her husband would never forget how I had helped them out when they needed it most. At a time that they were truly struggling financially I was in a position to offer odd jobs and such to help supplement their income and help them get through some very difficult times. Truth be told, I had not even remembered until she brought it up! But she remembered.

She shared with me how grateful they were for my assistance and how that same gratitude had turned her life around. That it was during those dark times that they were facing that she started to be thankful for every little thing, even when paying the bills. She told me that by finding all the greatness in their lives, even in the smallest details, they started to realize that not only that they had so much but that more and more was being drawn to them. I am happy to say, that today they own a wonderfully successful villa in Mexico and are living the dream. Remaining in complete gratitude and never taking one moment of it all for granted!

This experience inspired me to learn how to shift my view of myself and my life I went from living from the perspective of ego to living from the perspective of gratitude and started to witness my life move forward in ways I never could have imagined. This was not an instantaneous change, it was a process, but a process that transformed everything about my life. Today I live my life in continuous gratitude and my life is three times more abundant than it was in 2009 in every single aspect and is increasing continuously.

By releasing my ego and living in gratitude I also let go of constantly controlling, perfecting and proving myself. I never realize how exhausting this was until it was gone. Everything in my life has improved since that fateful day, especially my relationship with myself and my Source. This ironically has affected every other one of my relationships for the positive as a result. I am happier, healthier and feel freer than I have ever have been and live in such peace and abundance all because I have mastered the state of gratitude. This is why I believe gratitude to be the greatest of all spiritual alignments and have made this the first step in my book.

Your Future:

So how does one cultivate a gratitude attitude? Here I will provide three ideas on how to increase your attitude awareness. As living in gratitude comes from your heart and your mind, these exercises should be implemented for 21 days in order to make a lasting change in your behavior. You can practice all three or just pick the one that resonates the best with you. If none of these suggestions do the trick, then feel free to come up with your own inspirational ideas or search the web to see what others are doing. At the end of the day, it doesn't matter how we get there, as long as we find a way to discover gratitude for all the blessings that life is offering us.

1. <u>Keeping a Gratitude Journal</u>

I have published a journal called "21 Days to Gratitude" that aligns with the teachings of this book. This journal is a 21 day directed focus approach to looking at various ways in which you can find something to be grateful for. It is designed as a step-by-step, day-by-day program that will not only increase the gratitude you find in your environment but also increase your awareness in how you show up to life. It provides as easy yet effective opportunity for you to keep a gratitude journal for 21 days and provides additional space for your extra notes. If this does not resonate with you then perhaps you would like to find another prepared journal that does or create your own using one of your favourite notebooks.

2. <u>Thankful Wakening</u>

Each morning as you wake take a few extra minutes to give thanks for the day ahead of you. Thank the universe for your sleep, your bed, the weather; anything that comes into your thoughts. Mindfully go through your day and think of all of the positive ways in which you can enter into each of your activities. Alternatively, you can do the same practices at night as you prepare for sleep. Review your day in hindsight and reflect gratefully on the events you encountered. Be thankful for your surroundings, your friends, family, pets or your job, whatever is in your world that makes your days better. As you go through this process you will begin to see your gratitude list get longer and longer and longer.

3. <u>Gratitude Jar</u>

Prepare a jar that creates a feeling of gratitude in you. The jar can be anything you want it to be. Fully decorated, simple in design, homemade, store bought, it really doesn't matter. As long as it resonates with you and you feel comfortable putting it somewhere easily visible (the visibility will serve as a reminder). Once you've prepared your jar make the declaration to the universe that once a day you will write what you are grateful for on a piece of paper and place it in your jar for 21 days (this declaration will give you a feeling of responsibility). Once a week review the papers that you have gathered and see how quickly your increase of gratitude will multiply.

4. Look for the Good in Others

I'm not sure why it is or when it begins or takes hold in our own lives, but our society seems to be really big on positioning ourselves against one another. As a result we tend to look for faults in others to make ourselves feel better. We judge others based on how they look, the way they dress, the religion they practice, the colour of their skin, the car they drive; the list can just go on and on! The irony of this practice is that in the end, we actually feel worse about who we are and isolate ourselves from others based on superficial impressions. For many years now I have adopted the practice of finding something good about the people that I run into throughout my day. Whether it is something simple as a piece of jewelry they're wearing, the way their eyes crinkle when they smile or the way they interact with others. Every person deserves to be seen in their best light and that is now a gift that I try to bestow upon others as often as I can; as a result I get the ultimate gift of finding how much beauty that I can be grateful for in the world around me.

5. Say Grace

Although saying grace as long been associated as a "religious" practice. It doesn't have to be. It is also a nice way to remember to take a moment to give thanks and show appreciation for the things you have in your life. The focus does not need to be food based or "God" based, it can really be about what you make it. It just creates a moment for mindfulness.

There are numerous ways in which one can increase the awareness of gratitude in our lives. The important thing is in finding the one that works best for us. There is so much magic in this world and it is just waiting for us to tap into it. The secret to opening the door to this pleasure is in finding gratitude. So find your gratitude, practice it daily and you will see the enchantment in your world expand.

"The spiritual journey should be a selfish journey
~Osho.

Chapter 2

LOVE THY SELF
Step 2

The Concept:

Often the last person we ever consider is ourselves. So many of us have been witness to so much negativity and dysfunction during our formative years that we struggle with major issues of self-worth. Unfortunately, this epidemic does not necessarily come from having a lower-class upbringing, these days; it seems to be the norm. Whether one was belittled, abused, neglected, or had high expectations put upon them, the messaging is the same. You are not worthy as you are. As our parents struggled to understand how to deal with their own perceived inadequacies and failed to authentically empower themselves it created a direct impact on how we learned to function as confident, self-assured adults.

We were not validated for who we are at our core being and thus we do not believe that we are deserving. We then move into the world so focused on either giving or receiving to compensate for our own delusions that we are unable to find a balance between the two. We either see others as being valuable but cannot see the same value in ourselves and continuously feel we need to self-sacrifice to earn the love we so desperately seek or we demand love and respect from others without any comprehension of how to give back. While seemingly different in their approach each of these actions sprout from the same emotion... fear.

In either case, we are so busy doing in hopes of being fulfilled, we tend to lose sight of who we are and what matters to us. We have no understanding of what love truly looks like and think that somehow or another it is linked to either earning or receiving, giving does not even fit into the equation. Which still does not define love in its truest essence but is a heck of a lot closer than any other action. The concept that to love is to just be is so abstract that it hardly ever gets any recognition. We have been so misguided by well-intended, yet misinformed information that we spin around in circles trying to do good only to feel worse and worse for it.

The golden rule of love thy neighbour has been about since the dawn of time. We have seen this concept from Babylon and Egypt to Greece and China. It has been written in the bible and the Torah and the same belief is found in Buddhism, Hinduism, Islam and Jainism. This rule instructs us to love others as we love ourselves. Or more clearly put, love ourselves so that we may then love others. This simple rule has been so misconstrued by religion that the message has become to be understood as love our neighbours above ourselves. Well what good are we to them or anyone else if we do not love ourselves first?

It has been scientifically proven that unless our cup is full we simply have nothing to offer others, yet we think that we need to give and give and sacrifice all in order to be worthy of love. To paraphrase Osho, "Beware of the do-gooders, for they are the most mischievous of us all. They may start by massaging your feet but eventually their hands will be up around your neck!" Do not mistake this statement as a belief that there is a mission of intent from the do-gooders, for they do not know what they do. They believe that they are being of service to others but the truth is, they are only attempting to escape their own suffering.

This is very dangerous for no matter how pure our intention, when we attempt to do good for others we can only ever be a reflection of who we are. If we are miserable then we can only give misery, if we are angry, then we can only give anger, if we are fearful then we can only give fear. It is not until we can fully release the ego and live in zero state that we can be in service to others.

Zero state is where we are attached to nothing. We have no

expectations and we are not tied to any outcome. We have cleaned all our negative emotion and are left with only love. This is also where faith begins. For when we create from love, which is nothing, and have let all of our expectations go, which is faith, things will always be as they should.

So many do not understand that when we do good for others before we have understood our self, we do not free them, we possess them. Unfortunately, we have all been taught to believe the opposite. We must go do good for others so that we may find ourselves and be of value. This is a trick, as the greatest of all sin comes in the form of possessing others. If we truly want to do good for others, then we must attend to ourselves first so that we may give completely and without expectation. Not this is the truest vision of love so I will say it again... to give love completely and without expectation. The only way we can truly receive love, is to be love, and only love.

It is also important to recognize that when we love ourselves we can bring forth our gifts with purpose and appreciation. Whether our talent is to be artistic, creative, mathematical or being good with people. Whether our talent is to heal, to teach, or to bring forth messages. It is our gift. We have been uniquely blessed with it and it is our purpose. It must be recognized and developed. That is the only way that it will expand. As Marianne Williamson says, *"Your playing small does not serve the world. There is nothing enlightened about shrinking so that other people won't feel insecure around you. We are all meant to shine, as children do."* How we shine, is by embracing our talents and sharing them with others.

The bible speaks of talents and how if you utilize your talents, oppose to bury them, they will multiply. Buddha says that your work is to discover your world and then with all your heart, give yourself to it. Wayne Dyer, Deepak Chopra and many of the modern day masters talk about how we cannot recognize the genius in others until we recognize it in ourselves. It is all the same message. We are not being conceited or self-centered by accepting our talents, we are simply accepting, acknowledging and becoming.

To reiterate my earlier message, Osho says that *"The road to enlightenment should be a selfish one".* For until we focus on ourselves and realize our true potential we are of no use to others. He even goes so far as to say that when we try to help others before helping ourselves we can cause more harm than good. My translation of his message is that we need to understand who we are. Develop our talents, our gifts and master them before we can offer them to another.

Equally important as a value of self-love is setting boundaries. Setting boundaries and being true to yourself is one of the greatest ways in which you can demonstrate your capacity for love. When we set boundaries around how others treat us, not only are we showing respect for ourselves, but we are also showing respect for others. For when we respect ourselves, we cannot help but offer the same.

Enforcing boundaries needs to be done from a position of self-love and not from a position of hostility in order for it to be effective. When we demand that we are treated in one capacity or another we create a feeling of aggression and people will respond to it either by ignoring it or by challenging it. Being grounded in a state of self-love when enforcing our boundaries we remain calm and clear and present a respectful attitude that is much more likely to be reciprocated. In circumstances when it is not, we can simply remove ourselves from the situation and send the offender off with love and good intention in our hearts.

The bottom line is this, our world and our life here is so much more than we can ever fathom. We need to welcome all that we are meant to be and trust that the universe will bring us to the destination that we were designed to arrive at. By embracing our true essence and not being afraid to let our light shine, we will bring more to this world than by holding onto the archaic man held beliefs that we should not be proud of the gifts we have been given and live our lives being true to ourselves before being true to others.

This is the reason why I originally chose love yourself as the first step in finding spiritual balance. We must take time to connect with ourselves before we can be of service to others. Learn first to be strong in who we are and what we stand for. Find within ourselves all the divinity that we are and cherish every aspect of it. Discover our perfection and fall increasingly in love with who we are every day. We must be our greatest love story. We are all unique and precious beings yet we never recognize it within ourselves. We often seek others to reveal it to us when it has been within us all along. All we must do is just simply be, and in that stillness, offer to ourselves our love, just as we would to another.

My History:

I was one of the fortunate ones that was raised in chaos. Yes, I said fortunate. For to truly love yourself you must first embrace that it is your journey that has brought you to the amazing human you are today. But I will talk further to that later.

I grew up in a middle-class home with 5 children (3 boys and 2 girls), an alcoholic mother and a father who worked out of town. We also had a dog and at any given time two or more cats. My mother was the oldest to 4 brothers of which the two youngest would often stay with us as well. My parents believed in an open-door policy and would always receive those who stopped in just to say hello or needed their ongoing support. To say that I grew up in a full house is an understatement indeed.

The age gap between my older brother and my youngest brother is 13 years and I held the position of the baby girl. My two older brothers were 18 months apart and wild. And I think that is putting it mildly! The antics and the fights that would take place between just the two of them alone would cause any family to be considered dysfunctional! Never mind the rest of us! My older sister was the responsible one. Being the middle child, she tried so hard to pick up the pieces and provide some order for my little brother and I who were 7 and 10 years her junior. When she went off to college, everything collapsed.

I also grew up in the 70ies where it was the norm for our parents to have a great social schedule which included epic parties in our house. Many Sunday morning's my little brother and I would head into the living room while our parents slept and got our buzz on off the left-over booze that was still left in the glasses that littered the room. On top of that, no body spoke, they yelled. Although my parents made a great attempt to provide us with some structure and good family values they themselves were so broken that they just could not keep it together. They divorced when I was 13.

As for me, I was a free spirited, adventurous, dreamy, and curious child. I wanted to explore and understand everything. I believed in magic and I always had high hopes, big dreams and a positive outlook. From a parent's perspective however, I must confess I was a little challenging. In their attempts to control me and keep me safe I received the message that I was not a good girl and that for me to be successful in life, I need to be someone else. I need to be practical, focused, realistic, responsible and in my view, very mundane. Especially when compared to my 'perfect' older sister. This messaging began to create such a profound self-doubt in who I was as a person and a lack of belief that I could ever be successful if I were to follow my dreams. This feeling of worthlessness continued to grow well into my early adulthood while I struggled to find my way.

All this self-doubt and perceived negative messaging played a significant role in who I was to eventually become but at the time it was very defeating and confusing. It affected every aspect of my life, my career, my relationships, my spirituality and most importantly, my love and acceptance of self. Every time I got a glimpse of my authenticity and felt the love and hope return, I would quickly question who was I to have these empowering beliefs and shut them down. The messaging that I received as a child had become so imbedded in me and the voice so strong that I began to become my own worst enemy. I gathered increasingly more evidence as to why I could not, should not and would not do or try anything that I became almost paralyzed. I continuously felt judged by others and never, ever believed that I measured up.

In having said that, I want to make sure that you all understand, it was never my parent's intent to embed me with this messaging. Their re-enforcement of this message only came from their desire to protect me and keep me safe. It was as result of my juvenile interpretation of their intent that these messages formed. Unfortunately, coming from such chaos, no one could recognize what was happening within me or had the means to support me in not taking this personal as they were all so consumed in their own insecurities and issues.

As I grew, I desperately wanted to fit in. I wanted to find the place that I belonged so that I would no longer feel so alone. So isolated. I used to get teased about being the "Run Away Bride" as I would alter who I was to fit in to who I was associating with. I was not grounded in who I was or what I liked and was so afraid of not being accepted, that I adapted. As I adapted, I grew further and further from my truth. Today I am acutely aware of who I am and what matters to me. I feel so connected to everyone and everything that I live in an abundance of peace and happiness. Fitting in is no longer part of my purview and yet ironically I now fit in everywhere I go. Such a cool concept! So how did I find the love within me and become the person I am today?

Your Future:

From the young age of 19 I knew that I needed to start re-framing the way I looked at myself and at life. For all the damage that my poor mother brought upon us with her own pain, she was an avid reader and had a great love of books. As a byproduct of this love, one of the greatest gifts she offered was her interest in reading the masters. She had many books by Norman Vincent Peal, Napoleon Hill, Zig Zigler, Bob Proctor and the likes.

One day I was rummaging through the bookcase I came across a book called "See you at the Top" by Zig Zigler. In that book, there was an exercise that Bob asked us to do. His request was simple. Make a list of everything that you like about yourself and write it on one side of the paper. On the other side of the paper write all the things that you do not like about yourself. Be honest about these characteristics as this is a very important step in learning to love yourself. Once you have completed your lists, create a new list by joining the two lists together but present all your attributes as positives. For example, if you are not a very kind person, on your list state that you ARE a kind person.

Create your list to look like this:

My name is_____ and I am...

List...

List...

List...

List...

24

And I like myself!!

Then sign it.

How simple and yet how powerful! Now place that list where you will see it every single day. Whether you read it intentionally or not, subconsciously the message will still get through to you. I posted mine next to my bedroom door. That way every time I walked out of my room I got a reminder of all the greatness that I am.

What I found to be the most interesting thing about this exercise is that you not only will you start to appreciate all the great things that you are but you will also start to transform all the things that you saw as a negative characteristic into a positive one. To illustrate this, one of the things that I wrote on my negative list was that I was not a very responsible person. I was always late, I never stuck to my word, I would change plans at the last minute and I would quit things without any notice. I was young, self-focused and irresponsible. I drove the people around me crazy!!

After posting my list though, it was not long before I started to notice that I naturally began to take pleasure in becoming more responsible. I started to put effort into being on time. I started to understand that the only thing that mattered was my word. I began to be more careful of what I committed to and made sure to show up for others when I said I would. Before I knew it, it started to matter to me that I saw things through. When I committed to something and felt good to not let others down.

Today I am probably one of the most responsible, respectful, and reliable people you could meet. If I commit to something I am committed. If I say I am going to do something I do it. I value my word and my integrity more than anything else. I have come to realize that, at the end of the day, it is the one thing you must have to live and work in a world where you have to live and work with others. And it wasn't just the responsibility that turned around, it was everything.

Now I am not saying that doing this one exercise will magically transform you into a vision of self-love and appreciation but it is an excellent start and it is where I started my own personal journey. There are many programs, courses, books and videos available to help you on this journey of self-awareness but just remember that there is no quick fix. This will be a continuous process of work.

However, the good news is that with each level of self-appreciation we achieve it will propel us into higher and higher levels of acceptance and understanding. As a result, we will grow and develop at an increasingly exponential rate and spend less time in the negative and more in the positive.

As an interesting side note. I had a friend question me about my list when I had it hanging on my wall so many years ago. When I tried to explain it to her she scoffed and said "that's stupid!" Today I have a very happy, successful life that continues to bring increasingly more abundance into my world. Unfortunately, she still struggles with self-esteem issues which have manifest into drug abuse and harmful behaviors and have resulted in her losing everything that is of value to her. I think this sad little story demonstrates clearly the important of placing loving yourself above all else.

One of my favourite reminders of self-love is a quote by Marianne Williamson, "Our deepest fear is not that we are inadequate. Our deepest fear is that we are powerful beyond measure. It is our light, not our darkness that most frightens us. We ask ourselves, "Who am I to be brilliant, gorgeous, talented and fabulous?" Actually, who are you not to be? You are a child of God. Your playing small does not serve the world. There is nothing enlightened about shrinking so that other people won't feel insecure around you. We are all meant to shine, as children do. We were born to make manifest the glory of God that is within us. It's not just in some of us; it's in everyone. And as we let our own light shine, we unconsciously give other people permission to do the same. As we are liberated from our own fear, our presence automatically liberates others". Thank you Marianne,! Thank you for posing the question, 'Who are we NOT to be?' What a brilliant perspective! Let your light shine!!

I spent so many of my younger years downgrading who I was and playing it small so that I did not overshadow others. I was convinced that if I was equal to or less than my peers that I would somehow be more accepted. I was so afraid that if I truly stepped over the threshold and embraced all that I had the potential to be that I would end up alone or worse ridiculed for thinking I was 'more' than I was.

As I removed these irrational thoughts from my mind and moved forward into my authentic self and started to experience increasing success, I became an inspiration to others. Many of my friends and colleagues tell me that it was my example that allowed for them to make changes in their life and have belief in their ability to be more. How wonderful! This just further demonstrates Marianne's suggestion that "When we let our own life shine, we unconsciously give permission to others to do the same."

Now here is another thing that I have realized, and probably the most important. My external relationships, have a direct correlation with how good my relationship with myself is. Which of course includes romantic relationships. The happier I am with who I am, the happier I am with others. I know that seems very obvious, but I am amazed at how many people get into a relationship in an effort to be completed by another or to improve their current life situation. This is no way to find happiness. When we remain true to ourselves we can then be true to others. What this realization truly highlighted for me is that my ability to trust myself is what creates my ability to trust others.

For clarification purposes, I'll share with you a conversation I had with my girlfriend a while back. After sharing with her the vulnerability I show to my people she said "yea, but romantic relationships are different, we have so much baggage we carry from past hurts. It is hard to trust again" That was the moment that I experienced what I believe to be my biggest realization to date about the power of self-love!

I am not the same person I was the last time I entered into a relationship. Thereby, who I choose and the boundaries I set will not be the same as previously. You see with each "unsuccessful" relationship we experience, we have the opportunity to learn more about who we are, what we are looking for and what elements would make a successful relationship moving forward. It can also allow for some self-reflection and appreciation for what we bring into our relationships. Subsequently, no relationship needs to be deemed as "unsuccessful" as it provides an occasion to become a more emotionally intelligent person as a result of each experience.

It became clear to me in that conversation, that when we shift the focus from whether or not we can trust another person to whether or not we trust ourselves and our ability to judge another, we become free. Therein lies the key! If you are right with yourself you will be able to take all of your previous experiences and make the correct decisions moving forward. Even if that decision will not be a forever decision, it will be the right one for you in that moment.

This is not just limited to our personal life either, but to all aspects of our life. We put so much emphasis on the person or situation standing before us, that we lose sight of our own competencies. When we respect ourselves first we can shift the focus back to ourselves and demonstrate our self-love. We show our faith in who we have become and choices that we will make today knowing that it comes as a result of trusting ourselves and having successfully learned from our yesterdays.

So in having all that to say, my message for you is simple. Trust yourself! Have faith in all that you have learned from your experiences, extend love to yourself first and don't be afraid to open up your heart to others. As when you do you become your own hero!

"No act of kindness, no matter how small, is ever wasted"
~Aesop

Chapter 3

LOVE THY NEIGHBOUR
Step 3

The Concept:

I always find it interesting how people can view themselves as loving when the objects of their affection can be so targeted. To love others is to love ALL others. Not to discriminate or judge but simply to love. The person that lives on the street is no less worthy of our love than the person we idealize on the big screen. Every single one of us is on this earth is here with purpose. We are all here to learn from one another and as such need to be grateful for the existence of everyone. We don't have to do big things to express our love we can simply walk through the world with kindness and compassion in our heart. Share a smile, open a door or listen to a story. It is in the smallest of these acts that can sometimes show the greatest of love.

I have always believed that in sharing a smile or referring to a person by name when you see it on their name tag goes a very long way. As we have no idea what is going on in another's life and we never know how our simple smile or personal gesture can mean everything to them. Maybe it is the only smile they received all day, all week. Maybe they are feeling that no one ever notices them and when we identify them by name it makes them feel acknowledged for the first time in a long time. Maybe that little bit of kindness that we offer or the brief story that we share provides them with some much-needed insight or affects them more profoundly than we can ever imagine. We just don't know. Yet for the cost of extending just a little bit of thoughtfulness we can change their world, and ours. For a moment, for a day or for a lifetime.

We believe that to make an impact we need to do great deeds, make grand gestures and create massive change. This is not the truth and in believing this, it will only lead us down the wrong path. We get so lost on thinking so big that we end up not knowing how to help at all and in the end, we do nothing and end up helping no one. Yet if we were to just love one another and feel free to share that love in the smallest of ways it then becomes greatness. There is an old African proverb that says "It takes a village to raise a child". The same can be true in loving others. It takes a village.

If everyone that we came across in a day met us with openness, kindness and love, just imagine how that would transform us. Then go a step further and imagine what we would radiate onto others. The effects of this chain of events would literally change the world. To each individual this goodwill offering takes nothing of them, however to the recipient it gives them everything. This is a perfect example of how just a little from all makes a huge impact on one.

I have always said that in our personal relationships if we could go outside of ourselves enough to always make sure that our partner's needs are being met and if our partners were able to do the same and always ensure that our needs are being met, then everyone's needs are being met in a loving and generous way. Conversely, if we are only concerned if our own needs being met and our partner is only concerned that their own needs are being met, in the end, no one's needs are being met and the relationship implodes. This same idea can be applied to all of those we interact with.

I know this concept may seem to simple and inconsequential when we look to the news and social media forums. All around us we see nothing but intolerance in our world. Terrorism, hate crimes and wars we see it everywhere we look. The racism and attacks seem to be increasing at an alarming rate. The world as it is reported is falling apart around us and we frantically feel that if we don't stand up for ourselves and our rights we are going to lose everything.

With fear, we quickly jump on a bandwagon of hate without even knowing the full story. We get all riled up and filled with opinion and injustice yet don't even really know what we are fighting for. We get caught up in the negative and we lose sight of the light. It is here that we need to shift our focus. My mother always said that if you want to change the world, then you must start in your own back yard. Which is very similar to Gandhi's wisdom "Be the change that you wish to see in the world."

All around us we can find those who are "being the change" in small and wonderful ways. If we switch our perspective and focus on the positive, we will see that there are people everywhere doing great deeds of kindness every day. I am sure you have heard of the "Tim Horton's pay it forward" stories, or how so many people are rescuing animals or using social media to raise funds when tragic events happen in people's lives. How students bring prom to their sick friends or how people are giving free haircuts or dry-cleaning services to the homeless to help them re-enter the job force.

There are so many that are taking what could be a negative experience and turning into a positive one simply by showing compassion for others. Spending a moment in their shoes instead of judging from their own. One of my favourite stories is of a man who, after being mugged by a younger man, offered his assailant his coat and then took him out to dinner. You don't think that experience changed both of their lives? How magnificent was this man's grace!! This world is filled with good people doing great things, we just need to release our fears and choose to look for these stories or better yet, create our own.

Now I know that we often encounter those that tests our patience, our kindness and our compassion. It is not possible to exist in the world without having to (at least on occasion) deal with those that do not rise to the same level of vibration as we do. However, every time we meet someone who is in contrast to who we are, it provides us with an opportunity to get clear on who we chose to be. Life will always offer us situations that do not align with how we ideally want to experience things, but this is not because we are deserving of these circumstances, it is because it brings clarity to who we want to be and how we want to live.

We often forget that we have choice. Especially when we are dealing with others. We must remember however, that how others treat us is not a reflection of who we are but of who they are. Conversely, the same is true of how we treat others. Thereby, each time we are faced with controversy we must ask ourselves, "Who do I want to be and how can I handle this situation in the best way possible to honour both myself and others?" I know our world is divided and it seems to become increasingly so. As I grow deeper in my own spiritual journey the clearer this division has become for me. As difficult as it is to comprehend, you must believe that this is a good thing.

In order to achieve growth, we must experience contrast, for it is in the contrast that we are able to determine our truths. The world does seem to be a place of turmoil but for all of those we see stuck in the darkness, there are so many more entering into the light. We all know that our enlightenment develops more in our times of challenge than in our times of peace. As more and more of us become aware, the greater our light shines. The contrast that our world is experiencing today can also allow for us all to experience great growth as we move forward if we chose to let it! As individuals, as communities, as nations and as human beings sharing the same world.

The times that we are in may sometimes feel as though any attempt to make the world a better place is futile. That all hope is loss. That things are just spiraling out of control and getting worse and worse all the time. The truth is however, is that we are in the perfect position to make great global changes. Changes that could alter the entire world for the good. For it is the contrast that allows us to know with certainly what we DO NOT want, so that we can begin to build what we DO want. It is time that the pendulum starts to swing back. Perhaps this time with the knowledge we now have, we can keep it in balance.

Collectively we are in the midst of experiencing one of the greatest shifts ever known to mankind. Have you ever noticed that with each horrific event we witness it creates an abundance of those who offer love, kindness, and compassion to others? More than ever people are getting involved. Whether it is with small acts of kindness or through grand gestures it all matters as every act of generosity and love attributes to elevating our global vibration. So you see, without hate we would not know love, without chaos we would not know peace and without darkness we would not know light. And no matter how dark it may seem, light will always find its way through.

My History:

My sister tells the story of when I was a wee little girl and we were out for a walk one day. As I held her hand I looked up at her filled with childish innocence ask earnestly "Why is there war? Why do people have to fight? Why can't we just all get along?" Although I do not recall what was going through my little head at the time to have asked such profound questions at such a young age, my sister was forever deeply touched by this moment. She could not believe that someone so young could have that kind of awareness.

Now I know that I have always had a soft heart. For I remember having a bed fully of stuffies when I was a child and my greatest struggle upon going to sleep was trying to get them all to fit in my arms because I didn't want any of them to feel left out. Someitmes I would cry myself to sleep because I felt that I had hurt one of their feelings by not choosing them to be the closest to me.

Another memory of my soft heart was of a doll that I received for Christmas one year. The most popular gift for girls that year was the baby alive doll. I wanted that doll more than words could describe. Imagine having a baby that I would have to feed, cuddle and change diapers for. I would be like a really little mother. I was so excited! Receiving the gift that I was sure was to be my desired doll, I ripped open the package in anticipation. Much to my surprise and my disappointment it was not my much desired Baby Alive doll but a silly ole Baby Bean doll. I feigned happiness for my parents' sake and sadly put the doll aside.

That night as I was lying in bed this sense of guilt came rushing over me unlike anything I had experienced before. It was not the dolls fault I realized. She may have not been the doll I wanted but that did not mean that she did not deserve my love. I scrambled from bed to find my little Baby Beans and apologize for my poor behaviour but she was nowhere to be found. I searched and search and nothing! That night (and for a few others) I cried myself to sleep thinking of that poor doll out there somewhere all alone and feeling unloved. Although I continued to search for that doll, I never did find it. I am not sure if my parents took it to teach me a lesson or not but if they did, they never confessed.

I share these stories with you because I believe that most of us come into this world with this intense capacity for love, compassion, empathy and kindness. Unfortunately, it is through our exposure to life that we lose sight of who we really are. The messaging we receive on who we should be and who we need to become leads us to believe that we are not able to experience life with childlike love and wonder, but it does not have to be that way. Jesus is quoted in the Bible as saying, "I tell you the truth, unless you change and become like little children, you will never enter the kingdom of heaven".

I believe that what this passage truly means is that if we have the same openness, acceptance and wonder as children do, we will receive the greatest of all blessings here on earth. Blessing that do not necessarily come in the way of monetary or personal gain that so many believe is the path to happiness. They come in the way of the man on the bus giving up his seat for you after a long day at work or the simple synchronicity of your day going better than expected or the butterfly lingering on the flower just outside your window while you sip a warm cup of tea. We are inundated with signs, blessing and gifts each and every day. We just need to stay open to receiving them and being part of bringing these offerings to others.

My children have always bugged me about my tendency to engage in conversation with others while shopping or standing in lines. They have always asked "Do you have to be friends with everyone?" I think sometimes they were even a bit embarrassed. I always responded by saying "Yes!" I would then explain to them that we do know what others struggle with. That perhaps my silly little conversations with them will change their day, week, month or year. That sometimes just the recognition of someone can alter a life.

Showing interest in another can go a long way and it is the least I can do to be part of the human race. When my boys were younger this conversation was often followed with a lot of eye rolling and yeah sure moms. However, my sons have grown in to very kind and compassionate young men so I guess something stuck. I truly believe that when you are willing, you remain open. There are always opportunities for you to impact others. Not to mention, it also opens space for others to impact you.

Not that long ago I had a bit of time to spend at one of my favourite malls in a city I often visit for work. During my shopping expedition, I was presented with three young women, each working at different stores, each with different life goals and of course each with their own unique personalities. I was surprised at how engaged these women were with me and was honoured that they wanted to share of themselves. I confess that I was a little reluctant at first as I just wanted to get my errands done, but once I shifted the focus off of myself and onto them, I was opened to such a lovely experience that day.

The first was a young woman pregnant with her first child. In our conversation, we spoke of health and fitness. I was able to share with her some of my secrets to maintaining youth and vitality and the importance in always honouring our bodies and taking good care of ourselves as women. Not just when we are young, but all throughout the entire aging process. I shared with her how we do not have to succumb to the norm and that everything in life is based on our attitude towards it. It was a fun, light, easy going conversation and she was very grateful that I had come in and shared with her that day. She said it was exactly what she needed to hear.

The second was a lovely young girl who wanted to grow her career to a place where she could travel and work globally. She told me that she studies abroad and that once her visa had expired she had to return home and is now trying to figure out how to get back to Europe. I shared with her my story of how I developed my career in sales by pure hard work and determination and how blessed I am in how it has paid off for me. I encouraged her to stay focused and never give up on her dream no matter what the naysayer may have to offer. I disclosed that one of my greatest tools for achieving success was gratitude. That if she always came from a place of gratitude she would be doubly blessed in her dealings. She was so excited about our encounter that you could feel her energy was bouncing everywhere. She made me promise to come back in to see her on my next visit.

The third was a lovely young woman who was working in a store that was not her usual location for that day. As she was helping me pick out a pair of sunglasses for my youngest son we engaged in conversation about parenting. I shared with her what lovely young men I raised and how truly blessed I was to have them in my life. We talked about some of the struggles I overcame as a single mom and how in the end, the gifts that I did provide them with, was beyond anything that I could have ever imagined.

I shared some silly stories of sacrifices that I made that made me feel terrible at the time but how those same sacrifices became some of their greatest memories. I told her that my life was living proof that when you come from a place of love you are always giving so much more, even when you think you are not giving enough. She thanked me for sharing and told me that my story was inspirational and one that she will always remember.

Now I did not set out to talk to anyone that day let alone share so deeply with three strangers. Yet somehow the universe, god, divinity (whatever name you want to call your source) put these girls in my path. Not only because I had something to share with them but because they had something to share with me too. I had the opportunity to connect with three beautiful young woman and was reminded of the potential that we all have to live life to our fullest potential. It was a lovey afternoon of connection for all of us.

You see, we cannot share with another without receiving in return. It's the law of Ebb and Flow. Ok, I confess that I don't know if that is a real law or not, but I think it should be. I could have kept to myself that day. Done my shopping and just gotten on with it like I often do, but look at all of the blessings that we all would have missed if I had not been inspired to be open. So, when I talk about loving others it is not only about acts of charity or big gestures or small gestures it is like I said in my opening paragraph. It is also just simply about being open and moving through this world with love in your heart.

Living in love does not just extent to the love of other either. Love is everywhere! It is in the stars, the sun, the moon. Love is in the trees and the flowers and the butterflies. Is in the animals, the wilderness and the mountains. Yes love is everywhere, but most importantly, love is in each and every one of us. I know that may sound a little airy fairy, but the more you can appreciate and find love in the world around you the more you experience in your life. We need to not look for love, we need to be love and we need to live in love. Love for all things.

Yes we are all born into this world, but it does not mean we need to be of this world. We can escape the chaos by choosing love. By simply changing our perspective to gratitude we will begin to experience more love and as our gratitude expands, so does our love. It is impossible to experience one without the other. We need to find gratitude for the things we have to do and fill our free time with the things we love to do. As we become more grounded in what makes us feel happy and inspired, opportunities will open allowing us to pursue those avenues. We will shift from being tied to this world to being free in this world, and in our freedom we will be able to bring others with us. That is our gift to them.

We can change the state of our world by simply focusing on love as a verb. Make it an action. Love one another. Find love when we share a moment. Experience love when we paint, sing, dance and create! Feel the love that flows when we look at our children, our partners, our pets. Our focus should not be on the wrongs of the world, but on the rights of the world. On the love that we can find amidst the chaos and confusion. For what you focus on expands. When we focus on love, we find peace, and when we find peace, we find our escape.

Your Future:

So where does one start in their journey of kindness to others and living in love. Well the good news is, that when you truly love yourself, like we spoke about in Step 2, that love easily begins to extend towards others. It is impossible to have truly honest and real self-love and not develop compassion and empathy for others. Love begets love! However, for those that would like to practice loving others with more intention I have some great ideas on how to help get the love flowing.

When making any change, it is always best to start small. Studies have shown that when we change our behaviors in smaller increments the new behaviors is more likely to stick than when we try to make a total transformation all at once. As I mentioned earlier, love does not need to be given in grand gestures, love can be given with something as simple as a smile or acknowledging a thoughtfulness that someone offers you. Instead of running out the door and trying to save the world, why not start with just showing increased kindness and compassion to those closest to you?

Sometimes it is the relationship with those who are closes to us that create the greatest discord in our lives anyways so I think it is a great place to start. We often get so caught up in what the people around us are doing for us we forget to take a look at what we are doing for them. Perhaps it is time to make a shift. One of my favourite adages is "seek first to understand and then to be understood". Or likewise, using an adaptation of Kennedy's famous quote "Ask not what others can do for you but ask what you can do for others!"

They say it takes 21 days to break a habit and 21 days to implement a new one. The same can be true for changing the habit of thought. Why not practice for the next 21 days to open yourself up to those around you and look at what you can offer opposed to what you can gain. In my experience this shift is a great way to begin to create a feeling of compassion and empathy for others. Remember however, that just because you changed your behavior, it does not mean that the recipient will as well. If you find yourself dealing with someone that no matter how hard you try to elevate the relationship they are not willing to offer the same kindness and compassion towards you, you then have the choice to walk away.

As my father always said to me "There is no point in beating a dead horse!" It is important to make sure that you take care of yourself first and above all, love yourself. This is not about becoming egotistical; this is about spending your energy where it is best spent. If someone is not treating, you with the same respect and consideration that you are treating them with, then it is time to put yourself first and decide if it is a healthy place for you to be. Nowhere in loving others am I suggesting that it become a self-sacrificing action. That is not love that is dysfunction.

Another idea is to keep a 'Kindness Diary'. Many people like this form of reflection. If this is something that appeals to you I suggest that each evening as you wind down from your day you jot down three acts of kindness in your diary. If you are interested in having a more directed format, I have created a 21 Days to Kindness workbook as part of my Zen Matters Workbook Series for you. This is a nice way to keep track of the ways in which you are finding to share with others. This process also encourages you to be open to opportunities throughout the day so that you have something to enter into your diary at night. Before you know it, your diary will be over flowing as what you focus on will always expand. Always remember, Love, it is in you to give!

"Vulnerability is not knowing victory or defeat, it's understanding the necessity of both; it's engaging. It's being all in."
~ Brene Brown

Chapter 4

THE STRENGTH OF VULNERABILITY
Step 4

The Concept:

We seem to live in a world where we fear vulnerability. We consider it a weakness, rather than as a strength. We believe that if we show vulnerability to others they will no longer accept us. What we fail to realize however, is that it is through vulnerability that we are actually able to connect with others. When we allow ourselves to be "all in" it allows others to do the same. When we move from a state of vulnerability to a state of engagement we remove the "shame" from our stories. Shame is a master emotion; it is the fear that we are not good enough.

Being brave enough to become vulnerable with others allows us the opportunity to feel acceptance and see that we are indeed good enough. That we are worthy. We all have our stories but we can all unite and heal together in our vulnerability when we are open to do so. Have you ever noticed that most types of emotional healing programs, be it therapy or recovery, are based in sharing our truths? That is because it works. Once we expose our shame it no longer feels as dark and heavy as it once did when we carried it around inside of us. Sharing our truths creates a crack in us so that the light can find its way in.

Imagine if our ancestors feared vulnerability, we would most likely not even exist today. It was imperative for our survival as a human race to be vulnerable with one another. We worked together as a community, understanding one another's strengths and weaknesses to determine who had the capacity to do what in order to help the whole. This is how we survived for millenniums. Some were leaders, some were supporters. No matter what your role or what your strengths were, there was no shame. We all left our ego at the door and lived to survive together. Our focus was not on ourselves but on the common goal of the whole. It is interesting to think that our ability to be vulnerable was actually a survival instinct in days' past whereas today it is one of our most commonly avoided emotions.

Throughout our 'evolution' we have somehow forgotten the importance of being seen for who we really are and the benefits of living whole heartedly. As time moved on we shifted our focus from the survival of all to the survival of few, mainly, the survival of us and ours. As we became increasingly independent and self-sufficient we established the belief that we don't need anyone. It is now considered a medal of honour to be so distanced from others that we appear to be untouchable. This belief, that through independence and isolation we gain power, is widespread. Yet, we don't have to look far to see the result of this mindset. The division can be seen on so many levels. Everyone from Nations to family members are growing further and further apart from one another.

Perhaps it is time we started to behave more in line with how our ancient ancestors did and work together to focus once again on the survival of the whole not of the individual. Albeit our ancestors understanding of vulnerability was most likely much more instinctual, there is something to be said for that. Perhaps if we could just be present instead of overthinking everything we might have a chance to be open and connect more. For the feelings of vulnerability we experience are a result of our tendency to overthink.

When we concern ourselves more with what others may think of us rather on being our authentic self it creates feelings of shame and poor self-worth. If we were able to accept our strengths, weaknesses, experience, mistakes as all just being part of our story instead of equating ourselves to what we believe others perceive us to be, we would relinquish all feelings of shame and unworthiness. The confidence and openness in which we would then be able to approach others with would result in nothing short of connectedness and unity.

It saddens me to see the disconnect and competition in the world today. I see so many trying to outdo one another. Who has the better body, the nicest clothes and the bigger house? This behaviour is pushing us further and further from one another and creating a society filled with insecurities. Insecurities that are never expressed but are hidden beneath the drive to amass more and more in hopes to quell the feelings of inadequacy.

Ironically, this cycle is driven by the need to connect and feel like we are 'good enough' to be a part of something. What we fail to realize in the insanity, is that by simply being and embracing our authentic self as good enough, we are then open to connect with others in a genuine and sincere way. It is only when we allow ourselves to be vulnerable, are we able to find our people and our place in the world. As Dr. Seuss so profoundly stated, "Those that mind don't matter and those that matter don't mind!"

Now I am not saying that having drive or ambition is not a good thing, nor that wanting to be healthy and in shape or wanting a nice home make one insecure. I am all about health, abundance and success. I believe that the world that we live in is unlimited and that we can all have everything that we dream of (more of that later). What I am saying however, is that be truthful in why you want to achieve what you want to achieve. Don't set goals in order to outdo another. Set them to fulfil yourself. Be real with who you are so that you can be real with others.

Happiness does not come from over compensating, it comes accepting; accepting ourselves and accepting others, as we truly are. People tend to get confused about this philosophy as we tend to misinterpret accepting vs. achieving. To accept oneself does not mean to stay stagnant or to accept our circumstances as they are. We are expanding beings by nature and need to continue to learn, grow and achieve in order for one to feel truly fulfilled. Accepting is simply about not feeling shame and embarrassment for our story and not judging others for theirs.

I find it interesting how some of the steps are all tied into each other. This correlation actually made it quite difficult to know which step to write about first. Although vulnerability is a significant key to self-love and to loving others, it is also a massive and scary step. To be vulnerable is to be courageous. So, if we can find a little bravery in loving ourselves and then loving others, perhaps the concept of vulnerability will not be so daunting.

The word courage is from the Latin word "cor" which means "heart". The original definition of the word was to speak from the heart; to tell your story with your whole heart. To be vulnerable is to simply have the courage to be imperfect and to not have any shame about our imperfections. It is imperative that we find the compassion to be kind to ourselves first and then offer that same compassion to others.

As I said earlier, we cannot practice empathy with others if we cannot treat ourselves with a little kindness first. Finally, to be vulnerable is to cultivate a connection with others. This is a result of our wiliness to let go of who we think we should be in order to be who we really are. Once we are able to accept ourselves for all that we are and openly share ourselves with others then we will experience connections and acceptance beyond anything we have experienced before and be able to live whole heartedly without shame or darkness.

My History:

One of the greatest compliments I receive today is on my ability to make people feel comfortable and accepted with who they are. Many have told me that they appreciate my friendship or that I have inspired them in one way or another. Often these statements come as a complete surprise to me because all I feel that I do is authentically show up. Now as grateful as I am that people feel this way around me, I have to confess that I did not always have this impact. Well at least for many years I did not.

As I shared in my Introduction Chapter, when I was a young girl I was very open and authentic. My energy was light and expansive. I was an explorer, an adventurer, a free spirit. I was always happy and enjoyed being around others. I had a big family and lots of friends in the neighbourhood (mostly boys) and was always ready and willing to play and be social. I lived with an open heart and was truly authentic in who I was and never stopped to consider anything different. Then life happened. And the one thing I didn't confess to in my little self-description is that I was also a very sensitive being, so when life happened, it happened hard. Little bit by little bit situations arouse that started to make me question my value and self-worth. The more I questioned, the more I focused inward until such a time that I completely disconnected from others.

My mother's abuse = chink. My sister's preferred connection with my little brother = chink. The boy I liked choosing my best friend = chink. Being picked on by the 'tough' girls at school = chink. My first love getting another girl pregnant = chink. Rejection = chink, teasing = chink, other's opinions = chink, lack of education = chink, failed relationships = chink, being a single mom = chink and of course most damaging of it all, my perception of myself = chink. On and on it went, each event taking another piece from me until I became horrified of vulnerability. I was so filled with shame and self-doubt that I kept all my secrets tightly held inside terrified that if anyone ever knew the truth, I would be alone forever.

I worked so hard to over compensate for everything that I believed that I lacked. My goal was to become completely independent and self-sufficient. I began to put all my energies on becoming perfect. I wanted to be the perfect mother, have the perfect home, be in perfect shape and have the perfect career. I was so driven by proving to everyone that I was so much more than, what I believed, they thought I was. I watched, I learned and I became as perfect as I knew how to be.

I wanted to show all the perceived naysayers that I was capable, intelligent, and strong, that I did not need anyone to make it in this world. Feeling in control became hugely important to me. The more I fought to become, the more I disconnected. My circle of influence became smaller and smaller and my ability to deeply connect with others was progressively diminishing. To the outside world, my life looked great! I got so good at giving people just enough to make them feel like they really saw me without really giving them anything at all. But in my world, I was alone, I was afraid and I was constantly battling my self-doubt. I was the great pretender.

One of the biggest blows that came to my fragile world of perfection came when my boyfriend of three and half years told me that he needed to move to Europe and peruse his personal dreams and that he had to do this journey without me. Now when I use the term "boyfriend" that does not truly explain how I felt about this man. At the time, he was my love. I honestly thought that I would spend the rest of my days with him. When he came home to share this news with me, to say that I was confounded was an understatement. What came as an even greater blow was when he said the words, "I will probably never find another like you, for you are perfect!"

Did you hear that!! I was perfect! Yet it still did not prevent me from being hurt or having my world devastated. It took me so long to recover from this event and for years as I struggled to move on, family and friends could never comprehend the loss that I felt. What they didn't understand was that it was not the loss of him that was so devastating; it was the fact that at the end of the day, being perfect did not protect me from anything. I was completely and utterly vulnerable.

In hindsight, however, this was probably one of the greatest learning I have ever been blessed with. In that moment, when I felt the walls of my perfect life crumble around me, and my heart shatter into a million pieces, I was forced to realize that perfection was not the answer. Like with everyone else in my life, I only allowed this man to see what I wanted him to see. Although he thought he knew me better than anyone, he only knew what I allowed him to know. I never shared with him my vulnerability, my fears, my weakness.

He only saw that I was strong, independent and capable. He knew nothing of the shame that I carried with me. I never told him of my past experiences, my hurts and my disappointments and how they affected me. Everything that I shared with this man was from a place of strength. Even when he told me he was leaving, I never revealed my true feelings. He had no idea how destroyed I was, for I simply sat across from him and said, "Well, if you are going to go, you better get packing."

It took me seven years to truly let go of this relationship but every second of the struggle was worth it. I understood more about love from that relationship failing than I ever could of if it had survived. I know it tormented those that were closes to me (especially my dad) to watch me go through it, but in the end, I am so much wiser, stronger and vulnerable because of it. I remember one of the final turning points to letting go came from my father. The poor man was so frustrated seeing me hold on for so long that he finally said to me in an exasperated tone. "Stephanie! This man did not love you!! If he had, he would still be here with you!!"

I could tell that it pained him so much to be so honest and open with me. I respected him deeply for the strength it took to be so blunt and forthright. I knew that this is what real love looked like. My father put his own fear of rejection aside so that he could speak his truth to me. Not only did this conversation provide some much-needed reality about this relationship that I had held on to for far too long, but it also deepened my connection with my father.

You see, we believe that we need to be careful about what we say to others so as to not offend but in fact when we do not state our honesties it is then that we offend the most. Now I am not suggesting being a jackass about it; but when you come from a place of love, there is nothing that you should not be able to say and when you receive from a place of love, there is nothing that you should not be able to hear. Admittedly, it took me a long time to figure this out. Luckily, I have had one of the best friends in the history of the world since I was a teenager. She has always been the one constant in my life where I can always be the real me.

Over the years our friendship has taught me the kind of connection you can have when you share honestly from a place of love. Thank God I at least had this example. For a very long time however, she was the only one that I trusted and I had developed this weird sense of loyalty to her that did not allow for me to develop deep connected relationships with others. We've moved past this now and it has taught me that the more love I give the more love I receive. Not only has my circle of girlfriends expanded but so has my love for her as a result. As I said before, love begets love!

I didn't realize how far I had come until I was having a conversation with one of my best girlfriends last year. As we were talking the subject of vulnerability came up to which she began teasing me by saying "And we all know how much you loooove being vulnerable!" My initial response was to say "Ooooh yeah, not at all!" but then I stopped myself and said to her "actually, yes I do!" I realized in that moment that I do allow myself to be vulnerable. I allow myself to be vulnerable often actually and I am really ok with that! Initially, she was a little taken aback but then I explained to her that I was vulnerable with her all the time. That I shared with her some of my truest self, just as I did with all of those that I have CHOOSEN to be closest to.

The amazing bond I have with my people is indeed a result of my vulnerability with them and my ability to create a safe space for them to be vulnerable with me. I also realized in that moment, it is because of my vulnerability with them that they love me as deeply as they do. And let me tell you, I have some of the most amazing people in my world!! But it wasn't always like that I had to learn to open up and let people in. Trusting others was at one time a massive challenge for me. I had no intention to let others see any of my weaknesses. I was so scared that if other saw the true me I would be judged, scolded and most likely even laughed at.

Living a superficial life was becoming increasingly difficult and lonely. As much as it scared me to let others in, I realized it scared me even more to live my life out alone. With this epiphany, I decided that I would begin to take little steps in opening up to others and become more vulnerable with those around me. It was a very difficult process but also one that taught me so many valuable lessons about connecting with others.

The first being, as my best friend in the whole wide world constantly reminds me of, is time in. Nothing can replace the simplicity of just showing up time and time again to create a strong bond. As you invest in people and openly accept them for who they are you become a part of their world. It becomes important for you to be there for them for the good and bad, and the more you show up, the closer you become. It is inevitable. However, this does not happen over night

I've said it before and I will say it again, and probably again and again, everybody is in such a rush these days. No one takes the time to get to know anyone anymore. We need to decide before coffee has even ended if we could have a future with the person sitting across from us. We size each other up based on our own perception and with very little information make life altering decisions. I am not sure in what reality that is beneficial to anyone. Now I know that chemistry plays a big part in the decision making process, even in friendships, but

I am here to tell you that I have a couple of very strong friendships that were forged even though there was a lack of chemistry for me at the beginning. With a little time in however, I got to see them in a different light and today I value what they bring into my world.

In time and with a systematic approach (I am a Virgo after all) I was able to start opening up and began learning how to be my authentic self (Not only with others, but more importantly, with myself). I found that the more I became my real self the more I understood who I was and what mattered to me. The more self-aware I became the more I attracted many wonderful likeminded men and women into my life. Today I have some of the most honest, real, vulnerable and perfect friendships anyone could ask for. Once you trust yourself and your relationships, a whole new world will open for you.

Your Future:

So how did I come full circle? How did I come back to the wide eyed, open and authentic girl I was when I began this journey? Short story, it was by choice. Long story, it was a process that consisted of many different learnings and realizations. To help you in your journey, I have put together 5 steps that can assist you to open up to your vulnerability.

1. Be honest

When I talk of honesty it has much more to do with being honest with you than with others. More often than not, the first person we deceive is ourselves. Our ego works very hard for us, trying to protect us from any and all harm. It creates story after story to justify situations or events in order to preserve our self-worth. We then take these perceptions into the world and try to connect with others. When we falsely connect we easily feel rejection, which stimulates our insecurities, which makes us feel pain, so we then withdraw so that ego can lick our wounds and create for us a 'better' story, so we can get back out there and start all over again. OMG, that was exhausting just to write!

So let's be honest, because nobody wants to stay stuck on this continuous circle of unhappiness and the only way to stop the cycle is to get real. So how does one know if they are being "real". For me this journey started when I began to focus on recognizing the congruency between my inner being and who I presented to the world. This concept can feel quite contrary to many of us as we have become so good at hiding ourselves and entering into the world wearing a mask. However, once we are able to bring these two faces closer to alignment then we are well on our way to authenticity. In learning this I even went so far as to emailing 10 of my friends letting them know I was doing a little experiment and asking them if they could choose 5 words to describe me. The feedback was very interesting and I was surprised to find that I was showing up more authentically and congruently as I thought I was.

2. Accept there are no guarantees

I have a plaque on my wall that I received as a gift from my sister that reads "Sometimes our only available transportation is a leap of faith," I love this quote so much as it reminds me that there are never any guarantees. In order to get to our next destination we just have to move and have faith that we are going in the right direction. My life has been filled with twists and turns and where I am today is unrecognizable as to where I ever would have thought I would be. However, I know that I am exactly where I need to be and am so incredibly grateful for it.

Some of my greatest gifts have been in not getting what I had set out to have. Over time I have come to a place where I can set an intention and then sit back and trust that the universe will reveal it exactly as it is meant to be. I was recently asked by my neighbour if 10 years ago I knew that I would be where I am today? I told him that where I am today completely supersedes any expectation I ever had for myself. And the best part is, I know that I have only just begun my authentic journey!

These days, when things do not go in the direction that I had intended I just trust and look for all the ways in which I can find gratitude in the situation and enjoy watching my life unfold in pure perfection. It is just simply amazing. There is great vulnerability in this, especially as an ex worry wart and control freak but once you can master it; the beauty of it is breathtaking. It is like every day is a new present just waiting to be opened. This certainly makes life a wonderful adventure!

3. Ask for help/clarity

It seems like one of the most difficult thing for human beings to do is to ask for help when they need something or clarity when they do not understand something. I know this has been a massive struggle for me. For some reason these, two circumstances makes us feel weak. I know for myself I had so much miss placed pride that I could never allow anyone know that I needed assistance. I would just trudge through whatever the situation feeling alone and filled with fear and worry and doubt.

I used to struggle with a severe case of anxiety and panic attacks. Some days this was absolutely debilitating. Yet apart from my mother, I did not let anyone see the world of distress that I constantly lived in. I kept my job, I took care of my kids and faced the world as bravely as I could. This went on for two and a half years and was exhausting. One day, I was put in a position where my fears were overwhelming me while in a public place and I had to confess my demons to a new friend.

It was with complete vulnerability and fear of judgement that I shared my story. When I was finished he just looked at me and said, "I completely understand. I struggle with severe depression." In that moment, I felt a connection to another person that I had not for a very, very long time. My shame was removed and replaced with a feeling of freedom. This was the beginning of breaking the chains that bonded me to my 'condition'. Today I am happy to say that I have lived anxiety and panic free for over 10 years and never took one dose of medication to assist in my recovery.

I began to experience that being vulnerable and asking for help was not a show weakness, but that it demonstrates strength. When you have the courage to share your story with others it allows space for them to do the same and creates an opportunity for bonding. This is also true for asking for clarity. When someone says something or you find yourself in a situation that you do not understand there is nothing wrong with asking for clarity. As a matter of fact, in doing so you show others respect because you want to make sure that you understand where they are coming from.

4. Don't take rejection personal

This was such a freeing concept to me. As someone who worked so hard to be perfect I confess that for many years I sought most of my validation from others. I would take the opinion of others very personal and feel hurt and rejected when I thought I did not get their approval, especially when it came to my father. This need for validation made me constantly feel like I was in 'work' mode. When I realized that others judgments and rejections were merely a reflection of them and not me, I was able to develop a stronger sense of self love and value my acceptance of who I was above that of others. You see, no one knows you as you do. Anything that they may think they understand is only a perception of who they think you are. Don't ever let this cloud the truth of who know yourself to be.

Today I constantly get ask where I get my confidence from. I explain it very simply; it came when I stopped giving a damn about what anyone else thought of me. The most important thing to me now is that when I look in the mirror at the end of the day, I am happy with who I see looking back at me. Today my desire to grow and achieve is not about anyone else but me. There is nothing more that I feel I need to prove to anyone. I am so comfortable about who I am and the direction in which I am going. I feel so connected to source through love and gratitude. My life is all about simply enjoying the magic of co-creation and seeing where this amazing journey will bring me and who I will connect with along the way!

5. Embrace ALL emotions

Now this is something I admit that I have always been good with. From a very young age I instinctively knew that when an emotion was present it was best to feel it in its entirety before letting it go. I am not sure why I knew this, but somehow, I did. It wasn't until years later that I discovered scientific data that backed up this belief. It has been proven that when we hold in our emotions it creates stress in our bodies which then creates higher levels of cortisone. Cortisone is a hormone that helps us when we need to quickly react to a dangerous situation. When we do not use the cortisone that is released when we experience a real or perceived threat it become toxins in our system. The result of this is disease (dis-ease). This is also the result of suppressing the positive emotions that we are experiencing as well.

When you embrace an emotion, you allow for it to freely flow through your consciousness, thus releasing it. Our goal as spiritual beings having a human experience is to live in a place of high vibration so that we can enjoy the journey of creation that we came here to achieve. When we hold on to a negative emotion or suppress our positive ones we are reducing our level of vibration resulting in the feeling of being stuck. This is what happens when we do not feel the flow.

When you feel an emotion just feel it. If you are angry, be angry, if you are hurt, be hurt, and most importantly, if you are happy, be happy!! Obviously, I am not suggesting that you express your emotions at the expense of others, but find a way in which you can feel them and release them for you own well-being. Emotions are not our enemies. They are essential and a very positive mechanism for us humans. They help us get in touch with what we are truly experiencing and can in fact be very cathartic. Embrace them, enjoy them and then release them. I think you will be surprised at how good it feels!

"The weak can never forgive. Forgiveness is the attitude of the strong."
~Mahatma Gandhi.

Chapter 5

FINDING FORGIVENESS
Step 5

The Concept:

In forgiveness one finds freedom. I love this expression. It is simple and it is absolutely true. All of our insecurities, neuroses, jealousies etc are bonded in our inability to find forgiveness. Yet forgiveness is often one of the most misunderstood concepts and as a result our society is wrought with emotional fragility. You see, there are two sides to forgiveness; the past (which often relates to others) and the present (which often relates to self). When we think of forgiveness the most common understanding of this concept is in the forgiveness of others, those who we feel have wronged us. Unfortunately time and time again we tend to overlook the power of forgiveness of self. For total healing we need to consider both halves in order to achieve the whole.

The human condition to hold onto the past deprives of us of the ability to live authentically in the present. When we do not let go of our past it causes us to repress emotions and shut ourselves off from genuinely experiencing the joyfulness that arises when we live in the moment. We hold on to our pains and disappointments as if they are some kind of a medal of honour, yet all that we are doing is keeping ourselves bonded to the person who has hurt us as well to our own insecurities and feelings of unworthiness.

When we do not live present we become self-focused and look inwards, comparing ourselves to others (and always coming up short).

When we live in the moment we focus on what is happening around us and expand our attention thus being able to see the beauty that surrounds us. If we can find a way to shift our focus from ourselves and the need to feed our ego, we may not experience such a negative impact from others.

There is a song by Motopony where the lyrics poise the questions; *What if I was never rejected? What if you all just knew the right time to leave? My judgment was never requested but what if you gave me exactly what I need?* If we can change our perspective from pain to witnessing the experience as a gift, not only can it release ourselves so that we may freely move forward into something that could be much greater, but we will also be able to find a peace within that could alter our existence on many levels.

When we talk of forgiveness we often focus on the forgiveness of others. There are two sides to forgiveness however, the forgiveness of those who we feel have wronged us, and the forgiveness of ourselves for all they ways in which we feel we have let ourselves down. Equally as important and equality as powerful. What often holds us back from finding forgiveness is that we believe that forgiveness is about letting our offenders off the hook, but it is not. It is actually about ourselves. For when we offer forgiveness to others, we are really freeing ourselves.

Think of it from this perspective. When we hold anger, hurt, frustrations towards another we feel all kinds of wrong in side of us. Sometimes this emotional darkness can even cause physical illness. We are filled with stress, which increases our anxiety, which increase cortisone and so on and so forth. All the while the object of these emotions is carrying on, living there life completely unaware of what we are feeling towards them. Often times if they are aware, they don't care and just continue to live on in their state of bliss.

Meanwhile, we are being eaten up in side over something that we are allowing to destroy us. Thereby we are receiving twice the negativity from the original offence. Where does this possibly make sense? When we can shift our perspective from forgiveness freeing the offender to forgiveness freeing ourselves, we will be much more inclined to practice this technique and let things go.

My History:

Forgiveness has always been an interesting concept for me. For years I believed that forgiveness was not an area that I needed to put a lot of focus on. Not that I didn't feel that I had a lot to forgive in my life. I mean really, just the fact that my mother is an alcoholic my ex is, well my ex, that would be enough for most. Now I am not saying that I am not a forgiving person either. There are time where I feel that I am too forgiving. I am just saying that due to the fact that I have always been a natural optimist, I have a tendency to either let things go too easily or to skim over my focus on them. To be honest, for years I never felt that I had a lot that I needed to find forgiveness for. Until I realized that I did.

For the most part I am a very forward focused person. So much so that I cannot even sit on a train without facing the front or I will feel sick to my stomach. So when it comes to forgiveness I often viewed it as something that was in the past. A place I did not want to spend much of my time in. Yet as I tried to move forward I would find that I would get bogged down by some weight that I needed to break free from. I started to realize that the only tool that could do the job in these circumstances was forgiveness.

I recognized these moments by the amount of anger that would rise up in me when I either discussed or thought about a specific person or event. It was interesting because as theses occurrences were not always on the forefront of my mind and these intense emotions would seem to come up out of the blue. I didn't even realize that had so much forgiveness that I had to offer. I also found it interesting how it was so much easier to forgive some people than it was to forgive others. It took me a very long time to figure out why this was. I would get so frustrated when after thinking that I had found forgiveness, it would flare back up at a later date. My relationship with my mother is a perfect example of this.

For some reason I don't have a lot of childhood memories before the age of 10, but the ones I do have were pretty positive for the most part. I remember my mother being beautiful and strong with an energy that drew people to her. She used to volunteer at my elementary school and all of my little friends would tell me that they wished they had a mother as beautiful as mine. Yes my mother was beautiful and captivating, along with many other things that I came to appreciate over the years. Yet the one thing my mother was not, was the one thing I need the most as a young child. My mother was not a nurturer.

I think the need for forgiveness with my mother began pretty much from the very beginning, we were just two different souls from the start. As her life began to spiral downward and she spiraled with it, she turned to alcohol and the chasm grew. I can't recall all of the times that I needed to be independent when all I wanted was for my mother to take care of me. Tucking myself into bed at night, making breakfast and getting myself off to school in the morning, taking care of myself when I was sick, taking care of her when she had a night of too much consumption. Even though I was constantly surrounded by others. As a child I always felt very alone.

My parents divorced when I was a teenager. It was a long time coming and no surprise to any of us. The crazy in my house just grew increasingly uncontrollable by the days. My three older siblings had moved out of the house to start their own lives when I was 10 years old, leaving my little brother and I to fend for ourselves. For those three years I became my mother's caretaker. I cleaned, I took care of my little brother, and I took care of my drunk mother, the workload never seemed to cease. My father took care of us all the only way he knew how to. He worked, which also meant he avoided.

I asked my father years later if he knew how mom treated me and the abuse that I had endured. His only answer was "Why do you think your mother and I fought so much?" This answer did provide me with some sort of comfort at the time but that changed over the years. Once I had children of my own, I just couldn't understand why he didn't have the strength to remove us from that house. This was one of the major areas that I had to find forgiveness for my father. And thankfully, I did.

As much as I wanted to stay with my dad after the divorce, I felt some strange sense of loyalty to my mother. I didn't want her to feel alone so I went with her and we moved to the city almost 2 hours away from my family home, my father and my little brother. I was hoping that with it just being mom and I that perhaps we would be able to create the relationship that I always wanted with her. Only after I moved I found out that she had a new live in boyfriend and I ended up, once again, being the one who felt alone.

In the four years I had left before I graduated, we moved six different times and I went to seven different schools. I was always the new kid. Sometimes that was a blessing and sometimes that was a struggle. Friendships came and friendships went and through it all I developed coping mechanisms that still serve me to this day. As I write this I witness the insanity that I grew up in but I can honestly say, I no longer feel it. Finding forgiveness has freed me from my past and has allowed me to look back and see all the blessings in disguise that I was being offered along the way.

One of the greatest of these blessings was my best friend who I met when I was 15years old. A friendship that would have never happened if my parents did not divorce, if I did not move to another city and if my mother was not an alcoholic. You see we met only because our mothers met in an AA program that they both attended. Ironically neither one of us wanted to meet back in the day but our mothers insisted. Although their friendship didn't last (nor did my mother's sobriety) 35 years later and my best friend is still the most influential person in my life and my love and adoration grows for her daily.

Once I became an adult and started to do the work I needed to do to move past my childhood it was not a surprise to me that I had to find forgiveness for my mother. What did become surprising though was how many times I needed to. You see, forgiveness does not just happen because you want it to. You need to practice forgiveness. Consistently. In the case of my mother I had to find forgiveness over and over and over again. The struggle, I came to learn, was not in offering forgiveness for the original sin, if you will, the struggle came because her behaviour didn't change.

You see, I did find compassion for my mother and her pain. I did forgive her for what she did not know or was unable to give. I did alter my perception of her to see her from her shoes and not from my own. Yet all of the forgiveness and compassion that I was able to bestow upon her did not eliminate the way in which she continued to treat me. So each time a new occurance happened. BAM! I was slapped in the face once again and all of the past came rushing up to greet me.

What I learned through all of this is that forgiveness comes in waves. Each time we forgive we let go of a little more until such time that we are completely released. The other thing I learned is that we cannot control how other people treat us. We can however, set boundaries and by demonstrating love and support, enforce those boundaries. In time this will either change the behaviour or terminate the relationship. Either way, by respecting yourself and the other party, you no longer lose a part of yourself in this process.

I recognize that I put a lot of emphasis on my mother in this chapter and while we have a much healthier relationship today, it was a long process. Our relationship ebbed and flowed a lot over the years. There was even a point where I intentionally did not talk to her for a year so that I could break free of the cycle and learn to set boundaries. Today I understand that our relationship is what it is because of who I have become, not because she has changed.

This awareness came to me when she finally quit drinking 5 years ago. Although our relationship had improved over the years due to the forgiveness that I had offered and the boundaries I had set, I still hoped that the root cause of our issues were due to the alcohol that had been such a big part of her life for so many years. I was really looking forward to seeing this change in her. One day however, as we were talking on the phone and I listened to her share with me the experiences she was having in her life I realized that this is just who she is. She will never be anyone different.

With this realization I knew that if I wanted to make the choice to have a relationship with my mother, then this is the woman that the relationship will always be with. Ironically, this revelation did not come with disappointment, it actually came with a sense of freedom. I finally stopped fighting for her to be someone different. My mom is my mom. Good, bad and otherwise, this woman has taught me so much about myself and who I am capable of being and for that I will always love, appreciate and respect her.

My outcome with my ex yielded a very different result. Although today I can honestly say that I have released all my anger and animosity towards him, I choose not to have a relationship with him at all. I will spare you the details out of respect for my children. However, what I do want to point out by mentioning this is that forgiveness does not mean we have to continue to have a relationship with the person that we feel offended by. We have the power to choose who we associate with and if we do not feel that those associations are healthy or contributing positively to our lives, then we can respectfully decline the relationship.

Where I have found forgiveness to have the most profound effect on my life however, was in forgiving myself. To let go of all the ways in which I had disappointed myself, that I sacrificed myself, that I gave a piece of myself, that I played small, lived scared, didn't show up, made poor decisions. I am sure you get my drift. We all make mistakes but how many of us truly forgive ourselves for the things we have done along the way in our journey of growth.

It has been said that I am a very focused, driven, A type personality (which I believe is more my adaptive style than natural style just as a mention). As a result I have always been very hard on myself. I explained in step 2 that for many years I sought the pursuit of perfection, which really put the pressure on. As you can well imagine, the lack of empathy and compassion I had for myself was immense. I always disappointed myself. I used to put myself down and call myself stupid when I messed up, yet once again and my overall attitude towards myself was very self-degrading. I tell you, it was not a very comfortable space to live

When I learned of the concept of self-forgiveness, it was truly transformational! But it didn't happen overnight. It was hard, it was painful, I shed so many tears and I had to apologize to myself for so many things. It took journaling, meditation, positive self-talk exercises, being present and increasing my awareness. I had to commit to these practices continuously. Sometimes I made great headway and sometimes I slipped back into my old habits, but little by little as a whole, I moved forward. And it was worth it! So very worth it.

By learning to forgive myself I was able to live free. I realized that I was a spiritual being enjoying a human experience and that all of my trials and errors where just that, trials and errors. That happiness does not come as a result of achieving a certain goal but it a byproduct of who you become in the process. One of the hardest concepts for me to accept along the way was that I am perfect as I am in this very moment. That is all any of us need to know. That who we are and where we are in our journey at this exact moment, is perfect! As it will be in the next moment and the next moment. As we continue to move forward with this openness we begin to make gains not in small steps but in quantum leaps. It is extraordinary!

Today my relationship with myself is stronger than ever. I have forgiven my baby self, my child self, my teenage self and my adult self. I have offered all stages and ages the unconditional love, support and compassion that we all deserve to have and I continue to do so daily. I enjoy my company, I appreciate my abilities, I encourage my growth, I follow my bliss and I hold no expectation as to where this will all take me. I just keep moving forward with what inspires me and it is awesome!

I know that this may sound a little narcissistic to some but it is actually the opposite. When we can truly and genuinely find love, forgiveness and compassion for ourselves as we would for others, it grounds us. In this grounding we are then able to extend the same to others. We are not self-seekers who are looking for the outside world to fill our cup. We are able to fill our cup so profoundly that our cup runs over with an abundance to share with others. Take a moment to consider the utopia in which we could live if we all found the capacity to do the same.

Your Future:

So where does your journey of forgiveness begin. I invite you to consider that when we are able to change our view point from pain to just witnessing, the experience becomes a gift. Not only can it release us to freely move forward into something much greater, but also offers a peace within that could alter our existence on many levels. In my experience, I have learned that when I readjusted my concept of forgiveness to be less focused on others and more focused on myself that is where the healing ultimate began. The greatest act of forgiveness comes in forgiving oneself as it is then that we can begin to forgive all others.

I have always found the act of writing to be very healing. Not only does it allow time for reflection, but I feel that once we commit our words to paper they become released. One of the practices I used in forgiving others was to write letters. I would sit in a quiet space where I felt comfortable and safe and I would write a letter to my offender and express all of my negative emotions. I would share what event I was reacting to, I would share what their behaviour looked like to me, how it made me feel and how it was not okay. I would then express that I no longer held on to this event as it did not belong to me, thank them for the gifts that I received from my involvement, offer forgiveness for their actions and release both myself and them from the experience.

When I was satisfied with my release I would find a safe space and I would then burn the letter in a metal garbage can. As it was burning I would say a little prayer for forgiveness and declare that I let this experience go. I would finish this exercise by saying thank you three times. Once for the offender, once for spirit and once for myself. I would then shake it off and go about my day feeling a little less burdened.

Another practice that I discovered more recently in my journey is the ancient Hawaiian practice of Ho'oponopono. It a cultural practice of reconciliation and forgiveness and in English simply translates to correction or making things right. Based on the theory of "you are in me and I am in you". The Hawaiians believed that we are all connected and as such are responsible for more than just our personal experience. They understood on a gut level that to harbor resentment against others hurts the person who refuses to forgive. By taking responsibility for how others show up in our world and by asking for forgiveness while sending back love, not only do we find healing for ourselves and our people, we clear the negative memories stored in our collective thoughts.

Dr. Ihaleakala Hew Len is the Hawaiian therapist who was responsible for bringing this practice to global awareness. His success in healing an entire ward of criminally insane patients without meeting any one of them warranted and investigation as to how he was able to achieve this. What was discovered was that through the use of an updated version of Ho'oponopono which he calls Self I-dentity, Dr.

Len was able to heal his patients through healing himself. Seems impossible, yet if we were to consider that everything that happens within your purview is your responsibility, then it only makes sense that you also have the ability to clear it.

There are four simple steps to the practice of Ho'oponopono., Repentance, Forgiveness, Gratitude and Love. It has been said that the order is not as important as the power of the emotion that we give to each of these focus points. Personally, I like to remember the order as I share it below as it has a cleansing flow for me. However, as I always say, you need to find what resonates with you in order for any of these concepts to be effective.

Depending on the area of Hawaii that this exercise is practiced, it can be done with three people in attendance, the two parties involved in the conflict and a mediator or independently. When practicing alone, we can simply "say" the words in our head while visualizing the person or event that we are seeking to forgive. The important part is in the power we give to the feeling and our willingness to the universe to forgive and to love.

1. Repentance – I'M SORRY

We are responsible for everything in our experience. As it is our mind that creates our reality it is what we see and what we put our attention on that becomes our truth. We tend to believe that our experiences are external. It is happening to us, not by us. We believe that everything is "out there.", but it is not. This realization can be confusing and perhaps a little painful at first but once you begin to practice this method on your inner self, you will notice how the awareness of your connection to "out there" increases.

Whether you want your first practice to be self-focused or focused on another all you have to do is choose something that you are dissatisfied about and say that you are sorry. Pull the situation or the person to the front of your mind and visual the cause of your hurt and simple say I'm sorry. If you want you can extend your sorry by including in more detail what you are sorry for but that is pretty much the whole step. I know it seems pretty easy, but I will caution you that you may be surprised by the emotion it brings up.

2. Ask Forgiveness – PLEASE FORGIVE ME

After you have done your apology it is time to ask for forgiveness. Asking for forgiveness does not necessarily have to be focused on a specific person, it could be from yourself, the universe or a group of people. Don't worry about who you're asking forgiveness from. Just say the words, please forgive me. Say it with the same powerful emotion and remorse you found in step 1 and don't be afraid to expand on what you want to be forgiven for.

3. Gratitude – THANK YOU

This is the step where you begin to feel the shift inside you. Say thank you. Say thank you and feel it in your heart as if you have just received the most wonderful and precious gift you could have ever received. Because you did. As I mentioned earlier, I like to say thank you in threes. One for the God in you, One for the God in me and one for the God in the universe.

4. Love – I LOVE YOU

Feel your heart open as you say the words, I love you. As you say these words visualize the light flow through you and allow yourself to resonate with the divine grace of love. Feel the love that you have for yourself, for others and for spirit. Stay here until you feel it is time to let it all go.

The most wonderful thing about this practice is that it always ends in love. Each time you go through this exercise you transcend into love. As your forgiveness expands and you release your negative emotions you will begin to see that there is so much love around you. And when you are able to live in a constant state of love, you will find that there is less and less that you need to find forgiveness for.

If you are wanting to have a more directed focus to help you with your forgiveness I have created a workbook as part of my Zen Matters Workbook Series to assist you with that. It is titled Finding Forgiveness and offers an opportunity to look into various areas of your life that may be holding you back from letting go of the past, finding forgiveness and moving forward with love.

*"Meditation is the soul's
perspective glass."
~Owen Feltham*

Chapter 6

MINUTES TO MEDITATION
Step 6

The Concept

Believe me, I know that life gets busy! To think that we need to make space in our busy days to make time to meditate can feel overwhelming. How does one find 20 to 30 uninterrupted minutes in a nice quiet place with the right mat, the right candles and the right music when we can barely find 5 minutes to eat? OMG! How stressful to even just to think about it! Isn't meditation supposed to counter our stress?

Well here is what I learned about meditation. Meditation doesn't need to be some grand gesture, it does not need to be time consuming and it does not have to have a big ritual attached to it. It can be as simple as prayer. A shout out to your higher self to make sure you are living in awareness and staying grounded as you move through your busy life. Now that is not to say that it can't be the big 20 to 30 minute ritual. It just means that you don't need to forego the practice all together if you are struggling to find time.

Meditation is really about taking a moment to free your mind, consciously connect with your divine being, get clarity about your reality and stay grounded in your life. When we look at meditation from this perspective, it offers the freedom to incorporate it in so many different ways. We can take a few moments before getting up, while we are in the shower, when driving, when taking the dog for a walk or when working out. Mediation can fit into so many of the tasks that we are already doing and is actually very easy to fit into our days. We just need to resolve to do it and be mindful enough to make it so.

No one really knows exactly when meditation was first introduced into our society. Some have suggested that it has been around for as long as we humans have existed and is part of our innate psyche. Scholars maintain that the earliest documented record of this practice comes from India and dates back to 1500 BCE yet archeologist have discovered carvings that suggest the practice dates back to 5000-3500BCE. Personally, I like the concept that it has been with us all along.

Records also indicate that there were three key people who were instrumental in spreading the practice of meditation. Many of us are familiar with Buddha, who began his practice of meditation in India. Some have suggested that he was responsible for inventing meditation but as I mentioned earlier, there are reports that date this practice far earlier in the timeline. Buddha's teachings however were fundamental in creating the practice of Buddhism and were equally as instrumental in spreading the value of mediation as a practice throughout the land.

The second key player in spreading the practice of mediation was Lao Tze. Also known as Laozi, which literally translates to "Old Master". Tze was a Chinese writer and philosopher and has been credited as the founder of the philosophical system of Taoism. A belief that references meditation and the idea of wisdom in silence. Tze's fundamental belief was that one should do nothing and in doing nothing one will follow the flow of events and not pit oneself against the natural order of things. That this is where we find our peace.

The third key player was a Dosho monk from Japan who travelled to China in the 7th century and studied Buddhism. It was also during this time that he learned about Zen and became influential in the development of the practice of Japanese Zen Buddhism. Upon his return from China Dosho became a priest at one of the great temples and is also accredited for founding the first mediation hall in Japan where one can practice the art of Zazen. Zen Buddhism is not a belief or a religion or a theory and it is not something that can be intellectualized, it is simply the personal experience of the here and now. Focused on the present moment, Zen Buddhism does not impose ideas or belief on its followers, it only offers a concept on how to think. Much like my intention with my writings.

It wasn't until the 18th century that that translations of these ancient teachings began to travel to scholars in Western Europe and meditation was introduced to the intellects and philosophers of the time. Making its way into the United States in the 20th century brought with it a new surge of interest regarding eastern spirituality in the west and contributed to what we now know to be the practices of yoga and meditation today. Although in the 60ies, it was considered to be part of the hippie movement, in the 70ies mediation became recognized in medical circles as having therapeutic benefits to stress release. In the 90ies however, mediation became main stream when Oprah Winfrey invited Deepak Chopra on her show to discuss his book "Ageless Body, Timeless Mind".

Today mediation is a common concept and a highly practiced exercise as a means to improve mental and emotional health. The benefits of meditation are vast and range from lowering blood pressure to releasing anxiety and from helping release addition to delaying and reversing age related memory issues as well as many other benefits that are also being touted. Research and medical communities continue to study the benefits of this practice and increasingly more finding are confirming the positive benefits for not just our mental and emotional health, but our physical health too.

Although there are many different styles of meditation and different ways in which you can apply it to your life, there are two areas that have traditionally been focused on as a practice. The first being referred to as **focused attention meditation** where you are invited to focus on a single thought, sound or image in order to clear you mind of its clutter and its distractions. This type of meditation often encourages you to focus on your breathing and is sometimes accompanied by a mantra or a calming sound. The second being referred to as **open monitoring meditation** where you are invited to observe the sounds in your environment and the flow of your thoughts. This type of meditation encourages you to broaden your awareness which includes any thoughts and/or feelings that you might otherwise suppress.

No matter how, when where or why you decide to give mediation as a practice a try, the benefits you will receive are numerous. The more that you are able to find time in your day for such an exercise, the more that meditation become a part of your everyday awareness. The coolest thing is, that once you begin to master this introspection through meditation, you will soon be able to quickly quiet your mind and raise your awareness even without being in a state of meditation at all. Thereby when issues arrive in your day to day actives, you find yourself being able to adapt your environment to your new level of consciousness in the present moment. Thus being less likely to be brought down by external forces. At least that is what happened for me.

My History

In the spring of 2007 I was working at my desk just after lunch when the phone rang. As I was talking to the caller my face began to flush, my heart began to race and my body began to shake. I did not know what was wrong with me, but I knew something was definitely not right. I quickly got off the phone and went into the washroom to splash my face with cold water and settle myself down a bit. It didn't work. I then found my way into my bosses office and as she turned to look at me she proclaimed, "OMG, are you okay?" Her concern only added to my condition and I quickly went downstairs to get some air.

Unbeknownst to me, she had my colleague call the ambulance in the meantime and moments after I went back inside to use the washroom I was having the door crashed in by a paramedic and an army officer. As I just about to faint from the stress from all commotion they put me on a gurney and wheeled me into the ambulance. I didn't even have a second to consider what may be happening to me. All I heard in the confusion was something about an allergic reaction.

Once in the emergency room they treated me for allergies yet there was no immediate change in my condition. The Dr. was somewhat perplexed as all of my stats were normal with the exception of the racing heart and weakness that I felt. After what seemed like hours, and a load of medication, I began to calm down and they sent me home with my sister. They had no idea what the cause was but none the less released me with a prescription for an epi-pen and some Benadryl.

The next day as I awoke from my drugged induced doziness the same experience began once again. There I was, home alone, with no idea what to do, what I could have eaten to cause this to happen and who I need to call. So I called 911. Within 10 minutes they had arrived at my house. Asking questions, checking my stats and inquiring if I wanted to go back to the ER. The only thing I wanted to know is what is happening to me and what can I do to make it stop. I was beside myself with fear. The kind paramedic that was attending to me simple said, "I think you had a panic attack".

A panic attack? The concept of a panic attack was so abstract to my consciousness. I had no idea what that even entailed. Up until that point of my life I had never had any kind of concerns regarding the state of my mental health. I mean sure I suffered from a little anxiety in my tummy during stressful situations and I did become a bit of a germophobe after the birth of my second son, but that was just normal, right? All I wanted to know was, what the heck is a panic attack and how do I get rid of them?

Well that day, I had discovered what a panic attack was alright. A panic attack was hell and so was all the anxiety that accompanied it. Nothing could have ever prepared me for the nightmare that I was about to embark upon. You see, I was quick to find out, that I didn't just get one attack, or even two. I was at the beginning of a journey that involved being diagnosed with acute panic and anxiety disorder and let me tell you, there was absolutely nothing cute about it!

For those of you who have never experienced a panic attack, let me explain it to you. Panic attacks begin suddenly and without warning. It does not matter where you are or what you are doing. You can be in a meeting, out shopping or driving in your call. They can even come on when you are asleep and you wake up in a fright all alone, in the darkness. Out of nowhere your heart starts to race uncontrollably, and as the blood flows to your heart to support this increase in beat rate it pulls from you extremities. You begin to feel weak. You start to shake. You are filled with a feeling of impending doom, danger or even death. It can also be accompanied by a shortness of breath, nausea, dizziness and detachment. It is scary, it makes you feel completely out of control and it leaves you absolutely exhausted after the fact.

The anxiety is generated as a side effect of the panic as you never know when an attack is going to hit so you live in constant fear of when the next one is going to strike. You then begin to worry about things that are unrelated to the base issue as for with anything, what you focus on expands. The worst part for me is that because the beginning of this was believed to be food/allergy related and my family Dr. continued to reiterate that message, I was afraid to eat. I was put on a restrictive diet where all I could consume initially was rice with the expectation that each few days I would add a new food item. The anxiety that I experienced each time that I added another element of food was intense to say the least.

It took every ounce of my strength to keep it together enough to hold down my job and take care of my kids. My room became my sanctuary and some days I would spend hours in there on a roller coaster of panic attacks rides. One coming right after another. On top of the panic and anxiety I felt a sense of shame which led me to distant myself from the outside world. I was afraid if I shared my issues with others they would see me as weak or sick. I suffered in silence. Only allowing a very close few to ever see my real pain. Even with those with whom I shared however, I never felt as though they truly understood what I was going through. I had never felt more alone.

Throughout it all I knew on a deep level that what I was experiencing was not a part of me and that I had to find the underlying cause. I refused to go on medication and I searched for outside assistance from holistic sources to find a solution to my struggles. I started to work with a natural path and received some help regarding my diet. Part of my treatment was with a Phycologist who worked with biofeedback and neurotherapy techniques and focused on balancing the Alpha Beta and Theta waves in the brain. They also taught me some coping mechanisms using the vagus nerve and understanding the parasympathetic nervous system.

Although I did receive some benefit from this treatment, it was over an hour away from my home, very expensive and was not covered by any kind of medical coverage. Unfortunately this only exasperated my stress levels at the time and I could not afford to continue. The other treatment I received was cranial sacral chiropractic care from a Dr. that was only 30 minutes from my home. I found this treatment very helpful. Not only was the treatment itself very calming, but my Dr. encouraged me to enter into a meditative type state while she was working on me. This was my first real introduction to the power of meditation.

Finding those moment of peace while in therapy prompted me to go in search of ways that I could find more. I researched, I read, I studied and I focused. As a side effect of the focus I found that I was able to take myself out of my anxiety for a few minutes and sometimes when I was really into something interesting, hours at a time. I know that doesn't sound like much, but during that period of my life, it was a massive relief. I began to take my meditation more seriously and be intentional in my practice. I was amazed at the awareness that I obtained from this training. I was able to even begin to recognize when I was attached to my human being vs. elevating to my spiritual being. Although this was not the end of my panic and anxiety. It certainly helped me to cope a lot better.

In total, I suffered severely for two and a half years. Although I learned coping skills I was never without the constant concern of when I would experience another episode. Which was frequently. Eventually I was able to get to a place where I would recognize one coming and use my heightened awareness combined with my coping skills to ride the wave and allow for it to pass. I tried to keep as calm as I could as I went about my days as I was afraid that even some excitement for something good would trigger an attack. I think the hardest thing for me through it all was that it changed who I was so drastically. I became a shell of my former self. I had lost my passion, my confidence, my laughter and lived in constant fear. Only to find out at the end of the day that the cause of it all, was my birth control pills. Can you imagine? Talk about a misdiagnosis!!

After stopping the pills the panic began to subside rapidly. Unraveling the anxiety took a little longer due to all the messages I received and beliefs I developed as a result of the information I received from the so called professionals. I started back at the gym (my original Dr. told me to stay away until they found a solution for me) and bit by bit reclaimed my health and started to put my life back together. When I went to see the Dr. that had been working with me for the past year to find a solution to my issues and told her that I believed that all of this was a result of my pills, she flippantly stated, "Oh that makes sense. I struggle with them too." After about six months of being off my pill and making tremendous recovery I saw an ad on TV stating that if you were taking these specific pills and had experienced any heart issues, contact the advertised lawyer. What a trip! As a side note, ever since that entire experience, I have not been a proponent of the medical system. I mean who can blame me?

None the less, this experience also brought with it many, many gifts. For the first time in my life I learned how to slow down, be present and enjoy the benefits of meditation. The time I spent studying and learning introduced me to some of the masters and the philosophies that have attributed to the life I live today. My awareness of self and my desires to share my story in an effort to help others also grew out of this experience. As did learning to be vulnerable and having to share my weakness with those around me. Which ironically helped me to connect with others on a deeper level and in a more authentic way than I ever had before.

Today meditation is an integral part of my life and I practice it in many ways. Sometimes it is a full on 20 to 30 minute guided session and sometimes it is a simple prayer or connection to God and my higher self. When I am really stuck on something I will even play a meditative video on the topic while I sleep so that my unconscious mind will do most of the heavy lifting for me. Whereas when I first came upon this ancient practice I felt so disconnected and alone, today I feel that I am fully connected and supported by my divine spirit, the universe and those who I choose to spend my time with. I trust the process and believe that my path will always take me where I am supposed to go.

I very seldom live in fear these day and when I do, I recognize it as reminder to reconnect and elevate my awareness. My ability to get from here to there mentally and emotionally has increased in profound ways and I spend more of my time being productive and engaged more now than I ever. I am now a very grounded person who lives in continuous expansion and excitement for what is next to come. I get told on a regular basis that people love my energy and my positive spirit and that they enjoy being in my company. I share this not as a boast, but only to demonstrate how far I have come. This is important to me because I believe that we all have the ability to overcome our obstacle's and live our life to its fullest (hence the books). I am certain that my ability to let go of the control that I so desperately sought, and free myself to live the life I was meant to live, was initiated in my practice of this ancient art of meditation. My hope is that it will bring you the same gifts.

Your Future

I believe that the first step to finding time to mediate is by increasing our awareness about meditation. It is really easy to overstep something that is not even on our radar so let's change that. One of the simplest ways in which we can do this is to take a moment right now and add some alerts to your calendar. Most of us have a smart phone today so why not make the best use of them. Think of all the time we spend using them to update our social media or to creep someone else's page. Why not set aside a minute or two to take a moment to breathe and connect. Pick a few times where you feel that you may be open to starting this practice that won't interfere with all the other super busy and important things that you've got going on and add some slots to your week.

Now let's look what we can do within these moments that we carved out. Wherever you are you can start by sitting up straight and closing your eyes. Then take 3-5 deep breathes to cleanse yourself. I personally like to do this five times as I feel it grounds me deeper. Feel your body rise and fall with each breath you take. As you breathe in, visual light and love entering your body. As you breathe out, visual negativity and darkness leaving your body. Once you feel relaxed allow your breathing to return to a normal pattern. If there is nothing on your mind then allow your thoughts to just float while you observe them. If there is a specific issue that you are focused on or request that you have. This is the point where you ask for assistance. Once you have done this repeat the words thank you three times and return back to the present.

I find that this exercise only take a minute or two and yet is a very powerful way to ground myself and prepare myself for an event or engagement. I often do this before an interview, a speaking engagement or even a difficult conversation. My request is that God will flow through me and that I will have the guidance and support to convey my message in a way that it is received as it is meant to be and will be impactful and inspiring to the recipient. I also do this before I sit to write. This exercise is beneficial if we are struggling with something as well, as we are inviting your subconscious or higher self to help find a solution. While this solution may not come immediately a sense of peace around the circumstances definitely will.

In this modern day of technology another option to bringing awareness to our mediation practice is by downloading an app. There are so many on the market today that will help us to find the right meditation program for ourselves. There are also many online courses and programs that we can sign up for. A common theme throughout my book is the 21 day program. We can find this to be applicable to meditation as well. The theory is that once we do something for 21 days it becomes a habit. They key is however, that once we break a day, we don't throw the entire program out the window, but that we resume again the next day.

Now if we are the type of person who cannot commit to something unless it is a tangible, then why not sign up for a meditation class where we can go to a brick and mortar at a specific time on a specific day of the week. The benefit of this is that not only will it become a part of our structured routine, but we are also open to the opportunity to meet other likeminded people. If there are not any programs that specifically focus on meditation only in our area, we can always take a yoga class. Yoga is a great way to practice mindfulness and meditation while providing your body with some excellent movement.

Now I mentioned videos a little earlier but I want to expand on that here. Videos are a great way to provide us with topic focused and guided meditation tools. Youtube offers a wide array of video that vary in content, focus point, delivery method and duration that we can listen to for free. It also offers morning specific mediations, nighttime specific meditation and sleep specific mediation. It offers mediation with a hypnotic element to them as well as ones that work with our beta waves. Whatever we feel resonates, I am confident that we will find it on Youtube.

The benefits and values of meditation are so main stream these days that it is literally available at your fingertips. There is no real excuse not to engage in this practice, especially when the benefits are so amazing. So here is to your journey to mediate. May you find the peace and happiness that awaits you!

"To bring anything into your life imagine that it is already there."
~Richard Bach

Chapter 7

MANIFESTING MIRACLES
Step 7

Now this is where the real fun begins. In this step we get to talk about the art of manifesting! That's right, the ability to create the life we want and have all of our dreams come true. Sounds a little pie in the sky, I know, but it is not. The concept of manifesting our reality has been passed down by our spiritual masters for centuries. The bible itself states in Mathew 7:7 to "ask and it shall be given, seek and it shall be found, knock and it will be answered." We can go even further back to 391BCE when Plato was quoted to have said "like tends towards like". So while the philosophy behind manifestation has been around for eons, it has now been proven as a scientific fact that we are capable of manifesting our own reality.

You can find the scientific backing behind this age old belief in various studies conducted by the biology, neurology and quantum physics communities. To understand the importance of this lets look a little deeper into what has been discovered in these finding. Starting with biology. The latest genetic research has uncovered that we inherit so much more than just how we look, our height, or what class we are born into. We also inherit certain negative beliefs and associations from our forefathers. This is one of the key reasons why we are not able to find success when we first begin to practice the art of manifestation.

As 40% of our personality is a result of our genetic makeup, we need to remove these limiting beliefs before we can really begin to get creative. The good news is that this in not insurmountable. Studies have shown that we are able to physically change our DNA through our thought actions. Our bodies and our minds are intrinsically interconnected. The thoughts that we think determine the health and expression of our DNA. Having this awareness will help you to identify in which areas you need to put some additional work into overcoming these blocks and open up your ability to manifest effectively. Meditation is a practice that can also assist with this and why it is such an important exercise to our overall wellbeing.

From a neurological perspective let's take a look at our mirror neurons. It has been proven that vibrating on a higher frequency and living our lives in a loving, kind and open minded manner will indeed bring more positive experiences towards us. The science behind this is based in the fact that we all have neurons that mirror observed behaviours. This fact allows us to prompt certain behaviours from those we interact with. So if we meet others in a positive manner that is what we will get in return. This is also true for the opposite. If we show up in a negative state, we receive negativity in return. Most of us do this every day on a subconscious level. Just imagine how our world would look if we put a little intention behind this. As the saying goes, "Like attracts like." Now we know the science behind why that is.

Evidence is also being gathered by neurologists to support the power of creative visualization. Studies show that those who actively participate in the visualization of their goals are more inclined to achieve them opposed to those who don't. This makes perfect sense as the premise aligns with a study conducted by Harvard University on goal setting. They found that after following a group of graduating students over a period of 10 years, those who had goals were more successful than those who did not. Most interesting though, is that those who took the time to write down their goals were the most successful of them all. It only makes sense that by adding visualization one would receive similar or even greater results.

Controlled studies have been done on the effects of visualization and increased performance with respect to athletes as well. For example, a study was conducted where three groups of athletes were asked to do three different exercises in preparation of shooting a basket. The first group was asked to spend 5 minutes a day visualizing making the shot. The second group was asked to visualize making the shot for 5 minutes and to practice making the shot 25 times. The third group was asked to only practice making the shot 25 times. All athletes were tested before the exercise to ensure their base meridian was calculated and noted.

After a week of participating in their respective "pre-game" exercise, all athletes were asked to shoot a basket. It is interesting to note that the group who only visualized making the shot had a higher success rate than those who visualized as well as practiced and those who only practiced. Many of the top performing athletes we know and love today claim that their success is as a result of practicing the art of visualization along with their sport. That they see themselves obtaining their objective before they even engage in the physical motion of the play.

A study was also conducted where it was concluded that people who attend they gym experience a 30% increase in muscle strength, were as people who only visualize going to the gym experience a 13.5% increase in muscle strength over a 3 month period. The science behind this is that brain studies show that thoughts produce the same mental instructions as action. Mental imagery affects the cognitive processes of the brain and as a result can improve motor performance as well as increase your self-confidence and prime your brain for success. All attributes relative to living your best life.

Add to that the support from the psychology community that positive affirmations not only change the perspective of one's life, but the repetitive pattern of this positive thoughts can change the chemical makeup of our brainwaves by creating new neural pathways Positive affirmations have become a mainstream part of recovery for various mental health issues. Another benefit of this exercise is the ability to eliminate self-limiting and self-sabotaging beliefs. Those who make positive affirmation a part of their lives are noted to have a higher satisfaction of life overall. So many benefits, and yet we have only just begun to talk about the application of all of this as it relates to manifestation.

Most of us have heard of "The Secret" or the "Law of Attraction". Both concepts have gained a lot of notoriety in recent years. Some of the attention these philosophies have received has been positive while some has been not so much. Although these ideas are great in concept and based in scientific findings, they do not convey the entire aspect to what it takes to truly manifest a good life. As a result, these practices are not effect for all or only effective for the short term. One of the reasons for this is the "do nothing" perception that they promote. My belief is that the true understanding of what it means to "do nothing" has been widely misunderstood and has been applied in the wrong sequence in this art.

The entire process of manifesting is in doing something. In addition to setting the intention (or making the request) and attaching the emotional feeling of it being actualized, we need to physically do the work to move towards the direction in which we set our objective. To think that we can just put out a thought out into the universe and have it magically appear is ludicrous. As Aesop was quoted to have said so long ago, "God helps those who help themselves."

I will use being a writer as an example of this. If I just sat in my bed and visualized being a writer, saw myself at book signings, dreamed of hosting launch parties etc. and never wrote a book, how would I ever realize my manifestation? If I do not actually write the book, I would not have the one thing that would truly make me an author. It is not the thinking that makes it so, that would make me a philosopher. It is the doing that makes me an author, the actual writing. There is not a power in the universe strong enough to make my vision come to fruition it I don't put the work in to making it tangible.

Likewise, if I hold the vision of becoming a successful author, while I write, open myself to source with visualization so that I can follow my inspiration, then I will be more liable to finish a book that will be success worthy. Once that is completed however, I still have more work to do. If I do not publish my book, advertise my book or reach out to others to let them know that I have a book available for people to enjoy, who will know that I have written a book at all? Finally, if I do not sell copies of my books and promote my message, how do I become a successful author? See what I am saying?

The problem is, most people don't want to do the work or they don't have a clear vision of how to get to where they want to go. They just dream of having a huge home, a huge life or whatever grandeur they focus upon and think that because of their visualization efforts, it will be so. They have no idea how to make it happen and think that all will be achieved by randomly winning a million dollars or the likes. Well the reality is, you can't even win the lottery without buying a ticket.

The other area of doing nothing where people struggle is in the ability to let go of the outcome and to trust the process. More often than not, once an intention or manifestation is set, people become obsessed with the outcome. They put all of their focus on how it is going to show up, when it is going to show up, why it is not showing up and so on and so forth. As a result they do not allow any space for the process to take place. The key in truly becoming a great manifester and living in a place of happiness and abundance is by letting it go. I am sure you have heard of the expression, a watched pot never boils? Yeah, it's like that.

Have you ever noticed that you can have a thought about something you want and yet have absolutely no attachment to it and then the next thing you know it appears in your reality? My first cognizant experience of this came to me in the form of a turret. You know, the round tower that is attached to many styles of Victorian homes? When I was a teenager I would always say that one day I wanted to own a house with a turret. Well after purchasing my first apartment on my own and completing the renovations, I was sitting in my Livingroom one day and realized that my living room was actually part of the turret that ran up the side of my building. It was so funny to me that I had realized my desire without even knowing that I did so at the time of purchase.

This is just one of the many examples I could use to demonstrate this phenomenon in my life. Recognizing this has helped me to fully embrace the art of manifestation as it should be and has helped me to create some of the most amazing realities for myself. You see the most interesting thing that I learned about manifesting is that I take action where others believe they should do nothing (after setting the intention) and I do nothing where others feel they need to take action (letting go of the outcome). The other experience I have by letting go of the outcome is that when we are not attached and just trust the process, the most amazing miracles begin to appear. More often than not the reality that ensues is far better than what we asked for in the first place. I often refer to these happenings as my gifts.

The other area that holds people back in effectively manifesting their dreams is where they hold their beliefs and doubts. If you have any doubts about your ability or worthiness of achieving your intentions then you will be dead in the water before you even begin. Likewise, if you have any underlying stories that you are telling yourself about your intention these thoughts could be acting as resistance to you creating your desires. For example, if I didn't believe in my talent and held questions such as "who am I to think I could help others?" that belief system would block me from achieving my desires and my manifestations would never become reality. It is important to work on eliminating any self-doubt or limiting beliefs as you move forward with this process. Whether those beliefs belong to you or to your family history. They need to be addressed before you can truly achieve success with this practice.

The art of manifestation is not for the faint of heart, and I mean that literally. In order for us to create the life we want, we truly have to feel it happening before it begins to unfold, not just wish or hope for it. The clearer we can visualize our desires and the more emotion we can generate in feeling it as it has already happened, the more likely we will be able to bring our desires into realization. Once we have set our intentions and have attached our emotions to it, we need then to offer the patience and space for it to appear. Becoming unattached to our desires is even more important as the emotion that we attached to it in the beginning. As we practice this exercise, the stronger our ability to do so will become and the more miracles we will receive.

My History

I became to be such a magnificent manifester that I earned myself the nick name of "SOURCEress" from my girlfriends. Because of my ability to connect with source and conjure things up so easily they began to questioned what I had gotten myself into. This ability did not come overnight however, and it is continuously approved upon on a regular basis. For as I learn, I grow.

I first learned of the Law of Attraction over 12 years ago. I remember attending a seminar where a gentlemen got up and spoke about how our thoughts can control our reality. As I had been doing self-work in some form or another for over the previous decade, I found this concept interesting and wanted to learn more. The idea that I could change my life by changing my thoughts opposed to doing all the work that I had done in unearthing my past offered an idea of relief to me. As I mentioned earlier, the past is not where I like to live as I am a very forward focused person. However, most of the books that I had read or the seminars that I had attended up until that point had a heavy focus on where my setbacks came from opposed to what I can do to move forward in a more positive direction. All this to say, I was willing and eager to do the exercises in the book that I had purchased on that fateful day.

I took the exercises in the book very seriously and diligently went to work to set to paper what it was I wanted to achieve. The book was very informative and helped me to understand that the words that I chose and the self-talk that I engaged in had a direct correlation to the level of success that I experienced in my life. Although I was committed in my practice of this new concept, I didn't really receive any life altering results at the time. I am sure in hindsight there were many little ways in which my life improved by learning this theory, I just didn't notice them as in my mind, I was promised something big to occur. I think this lack of success was due to the fact that I took a very cerebral approach to its application. While the Law of Attraction was a part of my psyche from that day forward, and from time to time I would pull it forward and put some conscious focus on this process, it wasn't until many years later that I really became successful in the art of manifestation.

Due to all the areas of personal development that I studied throughout my life. My situation was improving increment by increment. There are different learnings that I would contribute my success to, but nothing ever came easy and the path forward was always in small steps. Sometimes it was even a few steps forward and then one step backwards. I was beginning to feel that no matter what I did, I would forever be stuck in my status quo. What I came to realize however, was that what was truly holding me back was the negative attachment I held to where I came from, the belief that everything would always be a struggle for me and the narrative I had that frequently reiterated that I was undeserving. It was interesting to me that, although on paper I could give a plethora of reason why I deserved more, for some reason I just couldn't believe it in my heart. Try as I might, I could not bridge this disconnect.

That change for me came about four years ago. It was the day that I realized that my perspective was all wrong with respect to my past. That what I was holding on to was exactly what was limiting me in moving forward. You see I had so much shame about where I had come from. I detested the chaos in which I grew up in, I was embarrassed that I held no formal education, I felt judged that I was a single mother and of course, just to pile it on a little thicker, I felt defeated that I wasn't further ahead financially. It was surprising to me to find that I held so many negative emotions when I believed that I was such a positive person.

The revelation I had that day was so simple that it was at the same time so profound. What if instead of having shame of where I came from I could be proud of how far I have come? I considered that for a moment and realized that I did have a lot to be proud of. I created a life void of conflict and chaos, I had developed a great career despite not having a degree, I successfully raised two beautiful humans on my own and while I may not have been as far ahead as some, I was not so far behind as others. All in all, I had a lot to be pleased with and I was living a life that made me happy.

I am not sure where this thought came from as it seemed to have come right out of the blue but I am pretty sure it was spirit giving me a gift. From that day forward I felt free of my self-doubt and began to see myself in a completely new light. With this shift I began to make quantum leaps in identifying who I authentically was and going after what it was that I truly wanted from life. The more that I believed that I deserved the more that I was able to manifest. It was amazing to witness. The two other observations that helped in this process was that contrast is good and that when you let go of the outcome things move along much faster.

Nowadays when things don't go as planned or something comes from out of nowhere that conflicts with what I want, I don't see it as a negative. I see it as an opportunity to observe contrast. The concept of contrast is simple. If I don't like what I am experiencing, I bring awareness to what would I rather experience instead? When you are able to detach yourself from your experience enough to observe it from a positon of what you would like, it give less impact to what you do not want. In addition, it redirects your thoughts towards what you do want which makes your positive manifestation appear sooner.

As a self-confessed control freak, I admit that the practice of letting it go was a little more challenging for me than the other aspects of this exercise. The idea that I was going to trust anyone or anything with the outcome of my life was just such an abstract concept to me. I had spent my entire life learning that the only person I could really trust was myself. That if I did not control every aspect of the things that I wanted then it was never going to happen. So when it came to letting go of my dreams to some "unknown" source. Well that just was not well received by my little psyche. It wasn't until I came across a so called mantra or intention that I attached to my manifestations was I able to let go and to trust the process. It was simply, "I am open to receiving this or something better."

That one line changed everything for me. Firstly, it was a declaration to stay open. By consciously choosing to stay open I was able to bring so much more into my awareness. Secondly, it reminded me that I was in receiving mode, not in doing mode. I likened it to accepting a gift from a loved one. Thirdly, I had set my bar on what I was willing to accept and created space for it to be better than what I had intended. This not only set boundaries that I would not accept something that did not align with me, this also provided an opening to view the things that did show up with a little more depth. I was then able to see what the gifts were that each experience bought opposed to shutting them down right away because they did not come in the way in which I had expected.

This openness created so much peace, abundance and happiness for me. It allowed me to release the control that was keeping me stuck and live in more freedom that I had ever experienced before. Today I am so detached from the outcome that life just flows. I visualize what I want, I put my action plan into place, I follow my intuition and trust that it will lead me on the path that will take me to my dreams. I also know, that if one door does not open, then it only means there is another down the road that will take to someplace so much better than the first one ever possibly could. And life is great!

Your Future

There are many methods being offered in which you can practice the art of manifestation. Some say you can do it in as little as 3 steps whereas others have as much as 13 processes involved. Personally, I have 7. Not only do the steps I list below seem practical to me, seven is a divine number so it makes sense that if we are about to make miracles, we should do so with divinity. So let's get you on your path to manifesting the life that you want and living in your peace, happiness and abundance.

1. <u>Get clear on what you want</u>

The first step may seem a little obvious but it is really important to be very clear about what you want and why you want it. Oftentimes we say we want something but don't have any real justification for doing so. Getting clear on what we want will not only help us to be more specific in our ritual but it will also bring clarity about what really matters to us. Let's say you want to have a nice car for example. Firstly, it is important to be really specific on what that car looks like. What is the make, the model, the year etc.? What is the cost associated with owning this car? Do you also need an increase in income in order to afford this vehicle? Once you have determined what the answers to those kinds' of questions look like, let's consider why you want that specific car. Is it for transportation purposes, is it about reclaiming something you lost in the past, or is it prestige and respect that you seek to find? Once you are able to face the truth about what is behind this desire, it will open the opportunity for you to see if it is really what you wanted at all.

It is also important to note that in order for this process to work, it cannot be at the sake of others or with the intention to bend another's will to your own. We need to be very mindful that we need to focus only on ourselves when creating our manifestations. For example, you cannot manifest that "Suzy" will fall in love with you. However, you can manifest that you meet the person that you recognize as the one. The person with which whom you would like to create a healthy, strong, loving relationship with and that she will feel the same about you. Now that may or may not happen to be "Suzy", as no one has the power to make anyone do anything. Remember free will?

2. Ask for what you want

When you ask for what you want be intentional with your words and evoke the emotions of what it feels like for you to be living the outcome of your ask. Visualize yourself in the situation of having your desire and feel yourself there. Perhaps you want a new home. Identify what that looks like, how big it is, where it is located and what style of design you want. Consider what it took to buy that new home. Did you have a realtor involved in the process? Where did you get your down payment from? How did it feel when you first walked into that property and you knew that it was the one. See yourself signing the deed. Feel what that felt like. Experience what it feels like to be living in that space. Feel the joy, the excitement, the sense of belonging. See yourself cooking, cleaning relaxing and entertaining in your new home. Make it as real, as tangible and as natural as breathing

3. Work towards your goals

What do you need to do to achieve your goals? What are the tangible steps that need to be taken in order for you to realize your dreams? Does it involve creating more income? Changing your diet? Altering your mindset? What does that look like to you? When you identify what needs to take place in order for you to achieve your goals you can then set a path. The important thing to remember however, is to follow your intuition as you move forward on that path. Your intuition will always be your guide. Act upon the ideas that come to you that make you feel good. If you are feeling inspired about what you are doing, then you are moving in the right direction. If not, perhaps it is time to reevaluate where you are headed and what it is that you are trying to achieve.

4 Trust the process

This is so important to being successful with your manifestation and yet it is one of the hardest things to achieve. Let go of your attachment and trust the process. Have you ever heard the expression "A watched pot never boils?" Well that is absolutely true with manifesting. When you look back over your life can you see how all the dots line up? That everything that happened needed to happen in order for you to reach the next step? Well that is also happening in forward motion too. If you are truly in alignment with your desires then everything will line up as it should. Your higher self has got this. Trust that everything is happening for your greater good and enjoy the peace that comes with knowing that everything will be alright.

5. Receive and acknowledge what shows up for you

Be a witness to what is coming forth for you. Don't hold so much attachment to what you want to receive that you are missing out on all of the amazing gifts that are showing up for you right now. Life changing events comes in so many ways. Sometimes it is in big ways, but more often than not it is simply a consequence of amassing a bunch of little changes. When we appreciate what we already have and acknowledge that it is enough, then we open ourselves to receiving so much more.

6. Keep your vibration high

As we discussed earlier in this step, our neuron mirrors are always at work influencing others and being influenced just the same. When we raise our vibration and show up in the world in a happy and positive sate, we will encourage others to respond in kind. As they respond in kind, our neuron mirror go off and also respond in a happy and positive way. The cycle just continues to expand. Everyone happily doing the neuron dance! As I said earlier, like begets like. Now I realize that circumstances can sometimes bring our vibration down a notch or two, but the interesting thing is, we don't even have to rectify the situation that brought us down in order to get back into a better mindset, we just need to switch our focus to something that brings us joy and live in that feeling for a while!

7. Let go of resistance

Resistance can come in so many different forms. Sometimes it is self-doubt and sometimes it is the doubt of those around us. Sometimes it is due to our negative interaction whereas other times it is due our genetic predispositions. Whatever it is that is standing in the way of our desires we need to recognize it for what it is and remove it from our psyche. For when we are able to let go of all resistance and allow the creative energy to just flow, it is then that we can truly witness magic in our lives.

As you can see from reviewing these steps, manifesting is not as simple as just throwing some thought up in the air and seeing what sticks. It takes clarity, intention, process and trust. It also is comprised of components that will help you to release limiting beliefs, encourage belief of self and live in a little faith. All of which naturally lead to an increased experience of happiness in one's life. So go on, give it a try! Happy manifesting!!

"Realize deeply that the present moment is all you have."
~ Eckhart Tolle

Chapter 8

PRESENCE: YOUR GREATEST PRESENT
Step 8

The Concept:

So many of us do not know the value of the moments that are right in front of us. We live our lives so focused on where we are going or where we have been that we do not understand that life is made up of the space that is right in front of us. We feel like time is running out on us and we live in fear that we will miss out. Yet by not focusing on the moments, that is exactly what we are doing. By living in an attitude of depreciation rather than appreciation we are using up our currency of life and spending our precious time wanting to be somewhere else.

Nothing is guaranteed in this life. We don't know what life will bring us in the next moment, the next day or the next hour. We have no control how others will react to us or how their choices will change our experiences. The only thing that is guaranteed is the present. This moment, right here, right now, at this time. We cannot live fully when we are always thinking of what "may" happen or what "has" happened. To live a fully satisfying and balanced life we need spend more of our moments being present.

I know this feels very counterintuitive to some as we have been so brainwashed to believe that success comes from having a superior ability to multitask. I certainly know I was! I became the multitask master (but more on that later). What we fail to understand is that when we are always multitasking we are never in the present moment. Our mind is always focused on what we have not done, or what we have yet to do. We are so busy thinking about doing that we cannot appreciate what we are actually doing in the moment.

Have you ever found yourself in a space where you are watching something on Netflix and a text pops up on your phone at the same time as someone walks into the room to tell you a "great" story? After about 2 minutes into the "great" story you realize that you have no idea what they are talking about, your missed a super important part of the show you are watching and you can't even remember who texted you? All of a sudden you are feeling a bit frustrated and just wish that you were just left alone to go back and enjoy your own space? I think we have all been there.

Now imagine if that story played out a little different. Your buddy walks in while you are watching your show and starts with his story. Respectfully you pause him so that you can stop your show and put your phone with the unanswered text down. You turn back to him and listen with intent to his tale. You both laugh and laugh. He walks away and you both feel that you shared an awesome moment. Then you turn to your phone and respond to your text. Once that conversation is finished and you once again feel that you connected positively to the person you were interacting with, you turn back and continue with the show you were watching. The best part being that you didn't' miss the most amazing twist that the story line took.

Same scenario, different outcome. Our relationships feel stronger. We are appreciated by others for our attention. We appreciate others for the gifts they bring into our lives. We are void of feelings of frustration which results in enjoying our personal time even more. All because we chose to be present opposed to attempting to multitask. It has been said that we do not have any control over what happens to us, but only in how we respond. When we are present we have the ability to respond to situations in a much more positive and proactive manner.

It is important to understand however, that when we talk about being present we are referring to being present in the moments that matter. There is nothing wrong with fantasizing about or planning the future we want. To be fair, this is a very important part of our success development and is a crucial step in manifesting our desires. It is equally as important to revisit our past from time to time. This allows for us to obtain the information required to grow and expand so that we do not make the same mistakes again. Our past and our future are both paramount to our spiritual growth journey. The key however, is to ensure that we do not live there. When you only focus in either/or, you are missing out on the incredible gifts of life. The magic moments.

When we remain present we are also less likely to be self-depreciating. It is only when we reflect on our past or consider our future that we feel that we fall short. When we are actively engaged in each moment we become unattached to our ego self and can just enjoy. It is when we allow our mind to wander that it begins to suspect, compare, and criticize. When our focus is fully on the task at hand or the person in front of us. There is no room for the negativity to invade. This is respect can be extended towards ourselves as well as to others

Another way in which being present is beneficial is in regards to our emotions. Emotions are a very important part of our experience here. They guide us, they protect us, they heal us and they inspire us. When you are able to be fully present with whatever emotion you are feeling it allows you to connect deeper with the message that it brings with it. You will be able to have a better understanding of how you are to address the cause of the emotion and discern whether your reaction is positive or negative to your environment. Being present offers the space to reflect before you engage. As is important to our physical health to acknowledge, express and then release our emotions, this awareness can help us with this process and allow for our emotions to flow through us quicker.

Did you know that being present also improves the quality of our relationships? Most people engage in conversation not actively listening to the person in front of them, but looking for an opportunity to inject their thoughts or opinions. The world is rampant of people not feeling heard and not feeling valued. Perhaps this is a result to the lack of engagement that we truly have with one another. When you can pause for a moment to really hear what the other person is saying, acknowledge their contribution and then respond in kind, your conversations and communications will elevate to a whole new level. Not to mention your bonds will increase exponentially.

As you can begin to see, the benefits of being present are numerous. As we become more and more present we soon find that all of our interactions become more powerful. Our connections become stronger and our relationships become deeper. Understanding that all we have is this moment helps us to make the most out of every one of them. We release expectation and embrace the unknown. I am not saying that we no longer have goals, plans, desires or focus on the big picture, we are after all cerebral beings. That is what elevates us from the animal kingdom. Well that and opposing thumbs, but I digress.

As human beings, we cannot be devoid of all thought. There are many times that we need to engage in active thinking. When working on a project, when communicating in an important conversation with a loved one, when planning or strategizing for an event, trip or proposal. We also need to just think and philosophize. One of the greatest gifts to our human mind is the ability to philosophize. To ask and to answer questions. While all of these exercise are thought processes, they are also take place while being in the present.

Some say that we have no past and we have no future, we only have the present. I personally believe we have all three. For if we do not have a past, we do not know where we have come from, if we do not have a future, we do not know where we are going. It is in the present however, that our life exists and when we can truly live in each moment everything else begins to take care of itself. It is by focusing in the moments we find peace and freedom. And that, is the greatest gift of all!

My History

I used to spend so much of my time thinking about the future and living in the past that I was hardly every present. Well more time daydreaming about the future and reacting to the past to be fair, but still, in the moments, I was nowhere to be found. What changed for me was the same thing that I contribute most of my success in life to. It was my children calling me out. There wasn't one specific occasion that I can attribute any of this to, it was more like an accumulation of many. My kids have grounded me in so many ways.

I remember one time while I was cleaning the house. I was always a mad cleaner. What I mean by that is that I would get mad every time

I cleaned. Now this didn't make any sense to me because the truth was, I actually enjoyed cleaning. It was kind of cathartic really. And I love, love, LOVE living in a clean space. Anyway, one afternoon as I was cleaning away, yelling at this, bitching about that, my oldest (who was about 13 at the time) yelled back at me "Why do you have to get so angry every time you clean?" This question totally took me by surprise. I had no idea I did.

Having been called out on this, I thought I would do a little introspective and see what the cause was. I realized that the reason was due to the anger and resentment I still held inside me to all the chores my mother made me do when I was a child. Once I realized this I actually found it a little comical and started to be more cognizant when I cleaned of being focused on the present and the satisfaction it gave me today. The interesting thing here is, that I didn't consciously take myself back during these times, I subconsciously drifted back because I was not focused in the moment.

When the boys were a little older, 17&13. I had to go out of town for work one week. I had just received a new position with a company that I had my sights on working with for a while. I was so excited to go, but at the same time very apprehensive about leaving my kids. I had never been away from them like that before. Before I went, I left them with a fridge full of food and one of my credit cards. After leaving them with the list of do's and don'ts and contact details, I was on my way. When I returned and walked into my home I noticed that although it was not a disaster, the house was not as clean as my standards were. With beaming faces my boys asked me if I was happy with the house. I immediately started to share with them they ways in which their cleaning attempt fell short of my expectations.

My oldest looked straight at me and said, "Please stop mom! We tried!" he then went on to say, "You realize that you left your teenage kids home alone with your credit card and you came home to no parties, no bad purchases and an attempt to clean the house? All in all I would say you are pretty lucky!" And you know, he was absolutely right. He was good like that! What he taught me was that when I walked into that door I was not present. I was living in my expectations instead. Had I been present I would have noticed all the gifts that my two amazing boys were offering me. The gifts of love, respect, trust and appreciation. Those are the gifts that matter, not my house be spotless.

As a single mom I had a lot of responsibilities. While I never felt burdened by these duties (I love being a mom) it did put me in a situation that I was not often very present. I worked a full time job, was worried about bills, was planning meals, playdates, Drs. Visits, extracurricular activities and so on and so forth. I became the multitask master! Just like so many other parents. But as my kids were growing so quickly and I began to feel the time slipping by, I realized that I wasn't always engaged. This realization scared me. To think that I had two of the most precious beings right in the midst of my universe and was not really connecting with them was heartbreaking to say the least.

I have always made a lot of time for my kids. My mindset had always been that I didn't have kids for someone else to raise. It was hard enough that I had to go to work and not be there for them afterschool. I wasn't going to spend our free time apart too. My friends used to tease me about the closeness I had with my boys. They knew, that if I was invited, my boys were invited too. Unless of course it was an event where minors where not allowed.

One story that I still makes me laugh was when I was invited to my girlfriends for a girl's night. The event happened on a night where I had already promised my boys that we would do a movie night. I told her that I would come to her party a little early so that I could be home for 9pm to hold my promise to the kids. She agreed and was happy that it would give us a little one on one. Soon after arriving she mentioned that she needed to head to the store to grab a couple things. She only lived a couple of block away from my house so I asked if we could just swing by my place to check in on the boys.

When we arrived at my home my boys were nowhere to be found. Although I was a little worried, it was early in the evening so I thought perhaps they were out riding their bikes. We drove around the neighbourhood a bit to see if we could find them, but to no avail. I told her as we were heading back to her place that I would give the house a call when we got in and if there was still no answer I would have to go. As we turned into her driveway, there were my two prides. The oldest one standing on the back of the younger one (who was on all fours) peeking into the window of my friends home. The sight was hysterical! My boys must have been 8 and 12 at the time.

We laughed and laughed and then invited the boys in of course. Soon after, some of the other women began to arrive. There I sat with my boys on our girl's night out. As each woman walked into the living room she would state, "I didn't know we could bring our kids!" One of the other mothers asked my youngest what school he went to, which led to if he knew her daughter to which he did. The next thing you know she when to grab her daughter from her house which then dominoed to another mom inviting her kids too! So our girl's night ended up being a family event for not just me and my boys but for a few of the other moms too. Needless to say, movie night didn't happen.

Over time and as I learned more, I started to put more effort into consciously connecting with my kids. To stop whatever it was that I was doing and to focus on their story, their project, their excitement. Now I confess, it was not always easy. I heard more about skateboarding, video games, cars etc. than I ever cared to (not to mention other things that I still have no desire to know) but I began to feel more connected with my kids than ever. I also learned that my kids were always far more present and connected to the moment that we shared than I was.

As a single mom, I never felt that I gave my kids enough. I think it is something that all parents may experience on some level or another, but for me there was also a financial component to it. I just honestly wish that I could have done more. One day however, I was given the most amazing gift that I had ever received from my kids. It was after my oldest had move out of the home and back to the city that we had spent the majority of our lives together. My youngest and I decided to go visit him for a week. For the entire time we were there the boys reminisced about all the things that we did together as a family.

As we roamed the city their beautiful little voices would yell out, "Remember when we did this mom? Remember when we did that? Remember when we went to watch the Whitecaps play, the Canucks play? Remember when we went to the aquarium, to 3rd beach? Remember when we went to see Dracula at the ballet, when we would go see movies at that theater? Remember when we used to skate at that park? Remember when we used to run in that trail? Remember when we went trick or treating in that neighbourhood? Remember when we used to live in that house? Do you know who much that house would have been worth now if you didn't sell it? Yup! My oldest always likes to keep me grounded.

The point is, my kids were always present. They always enjoyed the moments. They have great memories of their childhood. A childhood that included a momma that loved them and was always there for them. A momma that did give them enough. The gift they gave me that week was one of the greatest treasures of my life. Thankfully I was present enough in those moments to receive it.

Your Future

So how does one become more present in their lives? Being present starts with a fundamental shift from doing multiple tasks simultaneously to do the same tasks in sequence. By focusing on each task individually you are then able to give 100% of your attention opposed to a portion of it. This will not only make you more effective with the task at hand, you will also attain a healthier sense of accomplishment. This sense of accomplishment will also increase your self-confidence just as an added bonus. You can adapt the following three steps to help you make this transition.

1. Get grounded

Literally! Plant your feet on the floor! Visualize roots growing from the base of your feet and anchoring your body to the earth's core. You can do this while you are standing or while you are seated. You can even do this while lying in your bed. But if you are anything like me, you will be asleep before you get to the second step! Many professionals adopt a grounding ritual or power pose before they go on stage or into an important meeting. You can use this tool in so many areas of your life to increase your success.

2. Get centered

Once you feel that you are nice and grounded, close your eyes and focus on your breathing. Take a few deep breaths to help you get centered and clear with your energy. Notice all the thoughts that are passing through your mind. Don't engage. Just notice them pass by. When we are centered it is easier for us to live in more awareness of what is happening within us and around us. This awareness allows for the space to not immediately react to situations, which offers more control over how we respond and the direction in which we want the outcome to take.

3. Get connected

Now that you feel grounded and connected to your inner self, open your eyes and connect with what is in front of you. Whether it is a project or a person feel yourself truly connecting Stay present. If you find your mind wandering just call it back into the present. Listen with the intent to hear what the other person has to say and not only to add your input. Observe what is happening around you with appreciation and look for the beauty that your environment is offering.

As simplistic as these three steps are, they work! You can use these steps to set an intention before an activity or before your interactions with others. This steps also allow for you to consider your why in your tasks and connections. Understanding your why will help you to see the value in being present and thereby assist you in doing so. Being present also assists in you honouring your thoughts and feelings and extending that generosity to those around you. The more that we can elevate our awareness of self and participate in the world as kind, respectful and present beings, the more that we give to ourselves and to the world around us.

"When you change the way you look at things, the things you look at change."
~ Dr. Wayne Dyer

Chapter 9

ADJUSTING YOUR PERSPECTIVE
Step 9

The Concept:

Perception is describes as the mental faculty that allows us to assign meaning to that what we experience. Yet everything that we experience holds only the meaning in which we give it. Nothing has meaning in and of itself. Every situation, every comment, every action is meaningless until we decide that it is not. One could even go so far as to suggest that life itself has no meaning, and considered from this viewpoint, it really does not. Life is literally void of meaning until it becomes comprised of the meaning we give it. This is why mastering the concept of perspective is so important to creating the life that you want.

For every situation, we can find two or more points of view. For every book, each reader can discover a different story. For every situation, there can be more than one solution. For every experience there can be more than one take away. Nothing is ever black and white. To say that it is, only leads to limited thinking and as a result limited solutions. There is a huge grey zone and if perceived positively, it can be a very fun place to live. The more we live in the grey the more we can expand our thoughts and thereby our experiences. This becomes more evident as we increase our ability to see things from various perspectives.

It has always been interesting to me that two people can share the exact same experience and walk away with two different stories about what had just happened. More interesting is that the greater the time that has passed since the original occurrence, the greater the individual perspectives differ. This idea reminds me of a letter one of my best friends sent me when I was a teenager. In that letter he wrote something that I have never forgotten. It was a saying about perspective and it goes like this. "Two men looked out from prison bars, one saw mud and the other saw stars." This quote clearly demonstrates the power of perspective and is a simple reminder that things may not always be as we see them.

Understanding perspective can benefit us in a multitude of ways. One of the many ways is that it provides us with the power of choice. Perspective is a reminder that we always have a choice about how we want to experience an event or what importance we give to an occurrence. We can choose how we want to respond to something or how much energy we want to give it. We often forget that everything in our life is a result of the choices we make. Whether it is what we chose to eat, what route we take to work, or how we respond to an encounter. Absolutely every action we take is a choice that we make.

For example, say someone says something to you that you don't take very kindly to. If you were unaware of the fact that you have a choice and can alter your perspective to the comment, you may react immediately and be offended. In this insulted state you utilize a lot of your energy justifying how this comment is inaccurate and how wrong the other is for making this statement. This takes a lot from your emotional bank and leaves you feeling angry, hurt and energetically drained. This state can last for a much longer period than the original interaction and affect your entire day or even longer. You walk away feeling bonded.

However, on the other hand and with a little perspective, you realize that when someone is unkind in their comments, it is more a statement about who they are than who you are. As a result, you don't engage emotionally and you don't react with a negative attitude. You simply shrug it off and let it go or state that you are sorry the other feels that way and choose not to engage in any conflict. You then continue on with your day being unscathed by this encounter. You move forward feeling content, light and emotionally stable. Nothing escalated and no damage was done in the end. The engagement was quick and the effects did not stay with you. You walk away feeling free.

Perspective can also provide us with the motivation we need to get things done. If we are able to switch the way we view out tasks, they can become opportunities opposed to responsibilities. Think of all the things we "have to" do in any given day. When we think in those terms it results in us feeling exhausted and overwhelmed before we have even started the undertaking. Yet when we take a task and shift our perspective about it to something that makes it a desire rather than a demand, it feels lighter and becomes something that we want to do.

Let's use going to the gym as an example to demonstrate how "having to" do something affects our psyche. When we say that we have to go to the gym it feels burdensome. It becomes just another task that we have to do that we really don't have the time for. With this outlook, it is easy to put it off when something more "important" or more "enjoyable" comes along. The result is that we break our commitment to our health and wellbeing and end up feeling disappointed in ourselves in the end.

When we shift "have to" to "get to" all of a sudden our emotional attachment to going to the gym is altered and the burden becomes a pleasure. By positioning our thoughts as we "get to" go to the gym, all of a sudden the idea becomes one that is important and enjoyable. It becomes a priority to us and thus it is much more difficult to break the commitment. It becomes something that we look forward to doing oppose to something that we feel tasked with doing. It is amazing to me how changing one little word can have such a powerful impact on the outcome of our thoughts.

This same concept is true when we replace the words "I can't" with the words "I don't". When we say that we can't do something we feel like we are being restricted. This makes us feel like we are not in control and as a result do not place as much value on our decision to not follow though. It also makes us feel rebellious and sparks an attitude of 'we will do what we want to do!' We claim that no one can stop us. Ironically, even ourselves. However, when we use the words I don't, it offers a feeling of choice and we feel empowered. It makes us feel in control of our decisions. With this state of mind we are more likely to stick to our goals and decisions.

Our perspective is paramount when it comes to achieving our goals. When our goal becomes an opportunity opposed to an obligation, our brain has much more mental energy to make it happen. Having the right perspective taps into our willpower which thereby energizes us to move forward in the direction of our desires. Using perspective to identify our inspiration and using the right language to motivate ourselves, can't help but lead to more positive results.

Another benefit to perspective is being able to alter a negative into a positive. When something happens in our life that could be construed as a negative, we can change our focus and concentration on the opportunities that can be found as a result of the initial incident. I once met a woman who told me that she lost her house in a fire. As I was expressing my sorrow for her loss, she stopped me and said to not feel bad for her. She explained to me that while the situation seemed tragic at the time, it actually put her in a nicer home in a better location and her life has been much happier ever since. Although it seems hard to conceive, the fire was a blessing in disguise.

Yes perspective is pretty cool once you get the gist of it and it can be applied in so many ways to improve one's life. Yet I feel that one of the greatest benefits to understanding perspective, is that it provides us with the ability to connect with another in such a deep and powerful way. I am sure we have all heard of the saying "Do not judge another until you've walked a mile in their shoes." To me this saying is a perfect example of perspective and shows how it can help to develop empathy for others.

By seeing the world from another person's perspective we are able to identify with how others face their challenges, celebrate their victories and generally live their lives. It allows us to consider what matters to them and why. This offers a deeper insight into who they are, why they do the things they do and why they think the way they think. By gaining this perspective we can initiate more empathy and compassion towards them. This not only offers an opportunity for us to consider another viewpoint, it creates an environment where they feel safe to share more. This cycle of trust and understanding creates a stronger connection and builds better relationships.

This is why it is imperative that we choose our perspective carefully and make sure that we have considered all of the possibilities before making a decision or judgement. As we are all unique in our thought process, our emotional understanding and our ability to deduce analyses from each of the circumstances that we find ourselves in. It is impossible for any two people to have the same conclusion about an event. This is why there is so much miscommunication and so many disagreements in our relationships. When we can put ourselves in another person's shoes, it helps us to eliminate these conflicts. When you learn to look at a situation from a different viewpoint, it can completely alter the way you see things and open up new and wonderful experiences to discover.

My History:

True confession? I used to be an absolute control freak! I am a Virgo after all and true to my sign, I always wanted everything and every situation to go exactly as I had planned. Not only that, I also used to be a very black and white person, everything in my world was either one way or another. Things were either right or they were wrong. It was as simple as that. As a result of this thinking, so many of my decision were made with a quick judgement. The outcome would often be that I would find myself reconsidering my decision in hindsight and feeling that perhaps I was missing out on something more.

I am not exactly sure when perspective was introduced to me in a manner that I could truly grasp (as we are often introduced to something multiple times before we are able to understand how to implement it into our lives). I do know however, that once I figured it out, it transformed my decision making process and altered the quality of my life and my relationships. By understanding how perspective has such a powerful impact on how we see things I was able to broaden my awareness and consider all angles before drawing a conclusion. As a result, my choices today are much more solid and appropriate. Also, my interactions with others are much deeper and more impactful.

I remember a time when I was first acutely aware of how the power of perspective changed the outcome of what I was experiencing. It was not that long before I had to say goodbye to my father, although it was a while before he got sick. For some reason I was having issues with the fact that he didn't "protect" me from my mother when I was a child. After all of these years of never blaming him for what I had went through I was suddenly consumed with anger over why he had not done something to change our situation. I don't even know where this anger came from, but there it was.

That is one of the funny things about our emotions, things come up when we least expect it. Sometimes things we never even knew where hidden deep inside. For months I walked around full of anger, trying to figure out a way to confront him with the hurt and betrayal I was feeling. Although I didn't say anything, he knew something was up. He even went to so far as to ask my sister if she knew what was bothering me. No matter the vibe I was giving of to him however, he never failed to be there for me. He offered to help me in the ways that he could and continued to provide emotional support for myself and my boys.

I knew my distance was hurting him and it made me feel terrible inside but I also knew that my feelings were valid and that I had a right to explore them. As I did however, I was surprised to find how much empathy and compassion I was feeling for my father. I was able to see the situation from his perspective and I understood that he didn't know any better at the time. I could appreciate that from his viewpoint he was torn between trying to understand the anger in the woman that he loved and wanting to protect the daughter that he adored.

I was able to consider the pain and confusion that my father was going through at the time and how difficult the choice that lay before him probably was. I know it broke my father's heart to see my mother in so much pain, and I also know how much my father felt helpless in his attempts to protect me. Eventually my parents divorced. I think the struggle just became too much for my father. I had asked him once as a teenager if he knew what my mother had put me through. He simply stated that it was the cause of so many of their fights. I understood that in my father's own way, he believed that he was doing his best for me.

By putting myself in his shoes, I was able to let go of my anger and find compassion for what my father had gone through. I realized that his inability to do what I thought he should have done had no reflection on how much he loved me, but on the understanding and competencies that he had during that period in his life. I could empathize that he felt stuck and he didn't know what to do. He was never given the tools or taught the skills to prepare him for the experience that he found himself in.

With this new found perspective I was able to let go of my expectations of what should have happened and found compassion for what did happen. I no longer had to have a conversation to release my anger, for it dissipated with this understanding. I was able to return to the close loving relationship that I had with my father without having to revisit a difficult time in his life. In the end I feel truly blessed that this turned out as it did for unbeknownst to me during that period, his time on earth was drawing to a close. Lucky for me, I was able to spend what remained not dredging up the past, but creating as many new memories as possible before the day came that I had to say my final goodbye.

I received so many gifts of love from my father in those last few months. Gifts that I cherish every day. I understood more about the depth of his love for me in those final days than I think I realized over the span of my entire life. Imagine how much I would have missed if I was not able to change my perspective and went into that final phase holding my anger towards my father. In the end I was able to remember all the ways in which my father was a good man. Instead of focusing on a period of our lives where we were both living in pain, fear and confusion, I was able to focus on all the wonderful and amazing ways that my father was there for myself and for the rest of his family throughout his life.

We oftentimes forget that we are all just humans trying to be the best that we can be in this life. Some of us have more tools and some have less. Some of us have more knowledge and some of us have less. Some of us have more emotional EQ and some of us have less. And some of us have more pain to deal with and some of us have less. It does not matter where we are in our journey, none of us is better than another. When we can shift our perspective from ourselves and extend an ounce of compassion for another, the gifts we receive are awe-inspiring.

Shifting our perspective can assist us with larger matters, like the case with my father. Or it can help us with smaller everyday tasks like taking my dog out his bathroom break. I live in a three story walk up and talking my dog outside is not as simple as just opening the door and letting him out. I need to be dressed, he needs to be leashed, shoes need to be put on and outside we both need to go. Rain or shine, snow or sleet. This can feel like a massive chore at times, especially when I need to take him on his schedule, not mine.

It is seldom that he just needs to go for a quick relief either. It usually consists of him sniffing everything in the yard (for the millionth time), barking at strangers and wanting to take his time to find the perfect spot (insert eye roll here). This can make this task seem daunting and a pain the butt. However, by switching my perspective from a time waster to an opportunity to get some exercise my entire attitude about this process changes. It changes to the point that it even affects my posture and the way that I walk. Once again, small change, big result! There is a quote that talks about how the only thing we have control over in this world is how we react to things. I love this concept as it is the absolute truth.

Your Future:

There are many ways in which we can bring awareness to how we perceive things but in order for us to be truly successful we need to increase our emotional EQ. By increasing our Emotional EQ we are able to separate ourselves from the situation and see it for what it is opposed to how it makes us feel. Research has shown that we make better decisions when finding a solution for our friends' problems than we do when resolving our own. The reason for this is due to the fact that we are able to separate ourselves emotionally when the problem does not affect us directly and thereby consider more perspectives. This detachment provides us with better problem solving skills which makes total sense. Imaging how we could change the decisions we make for ourselves if we were able to implement the same detachment with our own difficulties. So before we look at ways to shift our perspective, let's look at ways we can increase our EQ.

Step 1 – Respect yourself

The first step in increasing our EQ is in understanding who we are, how we feel and what our triggers are. The way that we begin to do this is by pausing before we react. Most of us are conditioned that whatever happens around us needs to be met with an immediate response. This is not truth. We have the right to respond when we are ready to respond. Now I am not talking about ignoring someone or a situation, what I mean is that we can take our time to formulate the right solution. If you are in a conversation with someone and they ask something of you, you are not obligated to provide them with an answer right away. There is nothing wrong with taking a pause to consider your thoughts and/or your emotions before you respond. If you need more time than just a few minutes you can always offer that you will get back to them in a certain time frame with your answer. By not knee jerking to the situations that is before us, we can make better decisions and by default live a better life.

Step 2: - Watch your words

One of the most important aspects to how we show up in the world is with the words that we choose in our communications. Having awareness in this arena is beneficial to both your internal and external conversations. Increasing our awareness with respect to the worlds we choose is amazingly impactful. When we are mindful of how we communicate with ourselves and with others we can be more positive in our expression and more conscientious in our communications. It is important to understand that our self-talk is even more important to be aware of than how we talk to others. As a general rule we are often much more polite and respectful to another than we are towards ourselves. Altering our self-talk to a more positive position will allow us to be more authentically loving in all areas of our lives. An easy way to be cognizant of this practise is to simply remember, words matter.

Step 3 – Practise empathy

Focus on how others may be feeling by taking a moment to walk in their shoes. When you are able to view things from another's perspective you are able to generate more compassion and understanding in your interactions. You can also gain more insight into how others may be feeling by centering on the verbal and nonverbal clues that they give off. Another way to practise empathy is to consider why someone is behaving as they are. When you can consider what the driving emotion behind someone behaviour is you can help them to increases their EQ as well. Remember however, practising compassion does not excuse another from unacceptable behaviour, but it does allow for the acknowledgement and understanding that we all have our own issues.

Step 4 – Consider what you can learn

When you can look at each occurrence as an opportunity to learn, everything in your life will have more meaning. By looking at what we can learn we also are more apt to find the opportunities within each situation. Depending on our perspective, our experiences can either pull us down or propel us higher. As we increase our EQ we are more capable of turning misfortune into good fortune. By asking "what can I learn" we elevate ourselves to a higher perspective.

So now that we have some ideas about how to increase or emotional EQ, let's look at ways in which we can shift our perspective. One of the ways that I like to do so is by playing a little game call "The Other Side". Whenever I feel stuck in a situation I pause for a moment and consider "what is the absolute opposite of what I am thinking or feeling?" By going to the extreme opposite I am able to bring a brand new perspective to the forefront of my mind as well as open up the potential to consider all the ones in-between.

I played this game the other night with my partner. He was feeling frustrated with the lack of professionalism he was seeing in some of his colleagues. The conversation started by him venting about how their attitude affected him with his work. I invited him to stop for a moment to consider another perspective in how he reacts to this situation. I offered that perhaps if he were to look at his co-workers from a different viewpoint, he could find empathy in that they do not possess the skills and abilities that he does. After acknowledging this perspective he started to soften his attitude towards the people he worked with.

From there we brought it back to him and used this opportunity to highlight the ways in which he was a great employee and how he brings value that others may not. We were able to see that he was a committed and conscientious worker. We identified that he genuinely cared about his customers experience and was not just doing a job. We considered his ability to see the big picture and to understand what steps had to be applied to the process in order to achieve the greater goal. We also commented on his leadership abilities and how he could use this situation to utilize his given gifts.

This exercise not only increased his compassion for others and opened ways in which he could coach the people he worked with, it also helped to increase his self-confidence and acknowledge his skillset while doing so. The best think about playing "The Other Side" is that, as in the case of my partner, we were able to go even further than just seeing a different perspective. We were able to find multiple potential benefits to the situation. The more you are able to expand your mind and include additional angles to your outlook, the more positive the experience will become.

Let face it though, sometimes we don't want to have to go deeper, we don't want to consider new ways or come up with new ideas or solutions. Sometimes we are tired and our brain just hurts. We just need to just shut down and turn it all off. We are tired of always being on and elevating our awareness or considering another. Sometimes we just want to stop. We want to take a moment and make it about us. Yes, it is true, no matter how "enlightened" be become, we are all still human at the end of the day. The good news is however, we don't always have to get cerebral to change our point of view.

We can also change our mindset by listening to music that inspires us or by thinking about a situation that brings us joy. There is nothing that says that we need to stay in a negative state or situation or that the only way to alter our space is by doing a lot of work. If we can recognize that we are in an unhealthy place, we can utilize things outside of ourselves to raise our vibration. Then with an elevated vibration we are more open to consider different perspectives and enjoy more of what life has to offer. So if you need a change of atmosphere, consider taking a moment to think about something you might want to buy. I know this works for me!

Considering the big picture opposed to the current moment can also change our perspective. When we think about why we are doing something and where it is going to take us it can help us see more value in what we are doing in the moment. This can help take you out of the drudgery of the task at hand and help you to focus on the greater good of the goal. I know this may seem contradictory to what I wrote about being present, but I am in no way suggesting you live in the big picture, I am only suggesting that you keep in within your purview to make sense of why we are doing what we are doing today.

Making plans for the future is another great way to take us out of our now for a moment. Have you ever noticed that having something exciting on the calendar increases our happiness and sense of hope? I know that when I was planning my trip to Italy there was nothing that was going to bring me down. And when life happened, I focused on what was yet to come and it was awesome! It doesn't have to be big plans to increase our excitement either. It can be an upcoming date night, a weekend away with the family, attending a book signing with friends. There is nothing wrong with spending some time looking forward to what is yet to come.

Furthermore, there are a plethora of physical ways in which we can change our perspective as well. Just by standing taller and altering our stance we can change our entire physiology. Same is true by simply smiling. Did you know that the more we smile the easier it is for our brains to filter out our negative thoughts? Imaging that, just by cracking a smile. Smiling has also been contributed to being more attractive, reducing stress and elevating your mood. If it makes you feel silly to sit around with a forced smile on your face, find a good joke to read or watch one of the many silly videos that are trending these days and just smile. It does a body good!

Having a nap, going to the gym, getting outside and helping others are all great ways in which we can change our perspective and get outside of ourselves for a moment as well. One of my favourite things to do is take my dog for a walk or run in the trails out behind my home. I call it my Zen spot. No matter the season I find the experience to be peaceful and perfect. It allows for me to alter my state of being and recharge my batteries. I can't help but shift into gratitude every time I head into my trails. I come home feeling elevated with a fresh perspective on the day. The dog is pretty happy too. Just imagine all the new smells and the new friends he got to experience during our journey.

So no matter what path your chose to alter your outlook, always remember that you are never stuck where you are. We are free beings and have been given the gift of free will. As I always say to my people, use your powers go good, not evil. Perspective is such a great way to do so once you learn to master it. So don't go out there and try to change the world, just change your perspective and the world will change with you.

"The path to success is to take massive, determined action."
~ Tony Robbin

Chapter 10

TAKE ACTION JACKSON
Step 10

I know it seems strange to write a chapter on something that feels as aggressive as taking action in a book that is written about a journey to spiritual triumph. I mean isn't spirituality all about being calm and peaceful in our approach to life? As spiritual beings are we not supposed to tread softly along our paths in a quiet and gentle manner, leaving an abundance of love and blessings in our wake? Well not if you want to make an impact on your life that's for sure. We cannot attain spiritual enlightenment without doing something to attain it. Even if that something is to sit, meditate and do nothing!

Action and action alone is our vehicle for success. Life and the universe as we know it was created by cause and effect. Ever hear about the Big Bang? And if you do not subscribe to the scientific beginning of our existence, God took action by saying "Let there be light". Nothing in this world happens without taking action. Dreams do not become realities if they only remain as dreams. The writer does not share their story if they do not write. The athlete does not win the gold if they do not practice. The meal is not prepared if we do not cook. Anything that has ever come to fruition in this world only does so by taking action.

No matter what it is that we want, it is action and action alone that will make it happen. All the desire, spiritual beliefs and manifestation in the world will not yield any results if we do not take action. If we want to live a life that is more spiritually balanced, we have to take action to do so. We cannot just decide that we want this or that we want that and do nothing. It is in our action that our results will be determined. So let's take a look at why taking action is so important.

Firstly, taking action creates a belief in ourselves that we have the ability and the determination to actualize our desires. This belief in turn creates a confidence in our ability to go after what we want. This then leads to an increase in our personal belief regarding our worthiness. You see, when you put your time and effort into your goals, it produces a deserving mindset. You witness the work that you put into your project or task and value your own efforts just as you would the efforts of another. The more deserving you feel you are of your goals the more apt you are to achieve them. Action is also a way that others can see value in you and your belief. When you walk the walk others want to be a part of if opposed to when you just talk the talk.

Actions create habits which create success. Have you ever heard of the 10,000 hours philosophy? It is based on the premise that it takes 10,000 hours of deliberate practice of any given skill in order to become proficient in it. Now others have argued that we can achieve greatness in a much shorter amount of time but this debate is irrelevant to the impression I want to make here. The point is the importance of taking action. When we take action we are by default creating habits that facilitate our success. As Aristotle has been quoted to have said, "We are what we repeatedly do, excellence then is a habit, not an act." New actions initially take a lot of cognizant effort, but over time and continuously repeating the process, taking action itself begins to become a habit too.

Taking action identifies and eliminates what doesn't work or what we could be doing better. If we just sat around all day thinking about what we would like to do, we would never have the practical experience to understand if it will actually even work. One of the things that I have learned during my time in the business world is the important of the MVP. No, not the most valuable person, I am referring to the minimum viable product. Oftentimes people are so afraid to launch a product until it is perfected that the product never gets launched at all. By entering the market with a MVP, you can see what works and what doesn't' work and adjust as required along the way. By doing so you end up with not only a product in the market place, but a better quality product due to the test piloting that you did.

Action also creates momentum. With each step we take we create a forward motion with our project or objective. As we move forward we experience more and more success. In the beginning the task before us can seem very intimidating and it may take a lot of effort to propel it forward, but as we do, we find that it becomes easier and easier to continue. I like to equate this process to a Boeing taking off for flight. The majority of its fuel consumption and engine wear are due to it getting off the ground opposed to keeping it in the air. Same is true for us. The majority of our efforts are always spent in the beginning phases. Even in our relationships. Think about that for a minute!

Taking action also leads to an increase in opportunity. Have you ever heard the saying that luck is opportunity meeting preparation? When we take action we are preparing ourselves for when opportunity arises. By taking action we expand our knowledge, increase our skillset, improve our product or idea and meet new and different people. These people could potentially open additional doors for us or provide influence in one way or another that we have never even considered. Not to mention the opportunity that we will discover as we begin to grow and develop as a person. By expanding our awareness of what is around us, we will begin to recognize more and more the opportunities that already exist for us.

So while there are so many benefits to taking action, it does make one wonder why so many of us do not. Why do we stay stuck in our present circumstances and not put forth any effort to make changes to our lives. What causes us to live each day with the same routine as the day before? Never improving, never declining, just existing. It is not due to the lack of dreams, this I am sure of. I know we all have dreams inside us. Dreams and desires are part of our human makeup. Now some of us may have smaller hopes while others have massive visions, but every single one is equally as significant. So what is it that holds us back? Why are we not all out there trying to live the dream?

The number one thing that holds people back from achieving their dreams is fear. Yes that damn four letter word! Fear has held people back from going after what they want in so many different ways. It is the number one show stopper to living a life filled with happiness and abundance. If there was one thing that we could eradicate from this earth that causes more damage to the human race than anything else, it would be fear. Fear has stood in the way of people not only going after their desires, but it has also stopped people from communicating with one another, it has created separation, hate crimes and it has even created wars. If we could change our idea of fear from forget everything and run to face everything and rise, this world would be so much better off. As with everything however, change needs to begin at home. So let's look at how fear stands in our way of getting what we want.

Fear of failure is a pretty obvious one. We often times don't go after what we want because we are afraid to fail. The idea of not being successful in our efforts can sometimes be paralyzing. Our heads are filled with what ifs. What if no one likes our ideas, what if no one wants what we produce, what if people reject us or laugh at us? The perception of this pain becomes so real that we lay our dreams to die before they are ever even given any life. By taking action we can change our thoughts from what if, to who cares. When we take action we realize that we are in pursuit of OUR dreams. Not the dreams that warrant the approval of others. Besides, how many of those who laugh at us are the one who are pursuing their own dreams. None I'd bet! As Dr. Wayne Dyer always said "Don't let your dreams die inside you."

Now what about the fear of success? I know that seems a little counter intuitive as most of us think that we want our dreams to bring us success. But do we really? We all know that with more success comes more responsibility. Maybe we are ok with living our simple life, with little accountably. Maybe playing it small is playing is safe. Not to mention the fact that success will mean that we will probably have to re-evaluate our friendships. Not everyone in our lives today are going to be supportive of who we will become as we progress along our journey to triumph.

Some of the people you consider your closest friends today will reveal their true colours and you will find that there is no longer a place for them in your world. And that is perfectly ok! They were not meant to be part of your realm anyway. As you grow those who are part of your tribe will grow with you, those who are not will be replaced with others along the way. It's like what one of my favourite Dr. Seuss quotes has to say "Be who you are and say how you feel because those who mind don't matter and those who matter don't mind!" So don't let fear stand in the way of your greatness. The world needs what you have to offer.

Successful people know that it was their failures that propelled them forward much more so than their successes. Each time they fell, it was the process of getting back up that made them stronger. Each defeat lead to a deeper understanding of where they needed to make improvements and in what way they could improve their process. Coronal Sanders did not achieve success until after the age of 60 and after receiving over 100 rejections. By getting over our fears we are able to move forward in the direction of our goals with a clearer intent and in a more concise manner. When we can see our failures as just part of the process, they no longer become setbacks. Each time we get back on our horse, we learn some of our most valuable lessons.

Primitive messaging is another area that can impede us in taking action toward our goals. This is referring to who and what we believe ourselves to be based on the messages we received as a child. The saddest thing about the majority of the stories we tell ourselves or that others have told us are not even true. It is amazing to me how one event that happened to us as a child can be so impactful that we carry it around for the rest of our lives. So many of our adult decisions end up being based on this one moment in time. Now I realize that many of us have more than one moment, but even if we have a thousand moments, we need to put it in perspective and see that it is irrelevant to who we are today. As adults we have the ability to choose who we want to be each and every single day. Now that is empowering!

Then there is ego. One of my favourite topics. The great deceiver. The ego is a master at telling us a whole medley of BS in order to "keep us safe". The truth is however, it does not protect us at all, it only limits us. The acronym for ego is edge God out and it is with good reason. When you live in your ego there is no room for inspiration or for divinity. The ego's only goal is to avoid immediate pain and do whatever it sees fit in order to achieve this. The human need to avoid pain is so much stronger than the need to feel pleasure. As such, it is very difficult to rationalize that the temporary pain could bring long term pleasure when working on your goals. Ego feeds into our emotion and builds a case as to why we need to protect ourselves from what may occur if we go in a certain direction. Ironically, in the end, listening to your ego only keeps us stuck in the same old loop and ends up hurting us more. Ego will never be our ally, especially in taking action.

My History:

One of my favourite stories about taking action is the one about the drowning lady. I have told this story many times and have used it as good reminder myself as to why I need to take action and what that action could look like. The story goes like this:

In a small town in the southern part of the USA a terrible storm hit. As the rain poured and the water rose, an evacuation warning was sent to the citizens of the community. An older lady was standing in her living room as the water was flooding fast, praying to God to save her. Soon a man in a rowboat came by and shouted to the old lady, "Jump in, I can save you." The old lady shouted back, "No, it's OK, I'm praying to God and he is going to save me." So the rowboat went on.

As the rain continued to pour and the flooding increased, the old lady soon found herself on the second floor of her home. As she stood, up to her knees in water, a motorboat came by. "The fellow in the motorboat shouted, "Jump in, I can save you." To this the stranded old lady said, "No thanks, I'm praying to God and he is going to save me. I have faith." So the motorboat went on.

Before long the water has raised so much that the old lady was forced to climb onto the roof of her house. Sitting on the top of her home the old lady, cold and wet, huddled into a little ball. It was at this point that a helicopter came by and the pilot shouted down, "Grab this rope and I will lift you to safety." To this the stranded old lady again replied, "No thanks, I'm praying to God and he is going to save me. I have faith." So the helicopter reluctantly flew away.

Soon the water rose above the rooftop and the old lady drowned. Once she arrived in heaven she asked if she could speak to God as she wanted to understand why he didn't save her. When she finally got her chance to discuss this whole situation with God, she exclaimed, "How could you have let me drown God? I had faith in you but you didn't save me. All the years that I praised you and in the end you deserted me. I just don't understand why!" To this God replied, "I sent you a rowboat and a motorboat and a helicopter, what more did you expect?"

It is funny how the majority of us don't see the opportunities that are right before us and as a result do not take action when it is required. And I confess, that for years, I was just the same. Actually I was worse! I was a dreamer. I always has so many ideas of what I wanted to do and what I wanted to achieve but I did absolutely nothing about it. I walked around with my head in the clouds thinking that one day, just by happenstance, all of my dreams would come true. When I think back to the starry eyed little girl I used to be it makes me giggle. How perfectly naive I once was.

Don't get me wrong, there is still a little of that innocent dreamer in me, and I hope it is something I never lose. That is one of my qualities that pushes me to do things like write this book. I am glad however, that I was destined for another path than to just walk around all day with my head sky high. Life has definitely taught me that if you want anything to happen for you, you have to make it happen. Once I reached adulthood, it wasn't long before I figured out that I wasn't going to be discovered while eating in a restaurant. I wasn't going to be rescued by a wealthy philanthropist either. And I certainly wasn't going to be able to raise my kids on my own if I didn't find a way to take action.

When I was in my early 20ies, one of my best girlfriends moved to England. She married a man from Leeds that she met while vacationing in Australia. Yes Deb was a doer. I was always in awe at how she continuously made things happen. At the young age of 23 she was the manager of a trendy clothing store, had a cool apartment and a great car. I on the other hand, was still living at home, no vehicle and was working as a waitress while attending a shit collage. To me, Deb had it all! So when she was willing to give it all up to spend a year exploring another part of the world it absolutely astonished me. Her actions seemed inconceivable to me at the time.

No matter where Deb was living however, she and I always stayed in touch. Back in the day I was pretty good about writing letters and Deb always reached out when she came back into town. She was definitely one of my closest friends and had been for many years. So when she told me that they had decided to get married in England it pained me that I wouldn't be a part of her big day. Not that I wasn't invited, she wanted me to be there more than anything. It was that I knew I would not be able to go. England was just too far. It was too expensive and I was too scared to leave my home to visit another country. Although this hurt her, it was never about her. I was standing in my own way.

Over the years Deb would come back to Canada every summer and always make time to come spend a few days with me. It did not matter where I lived, she always made time to see me. While visiting she would regale me with her stories from England and encourage me to come visit. "My door is always open to you", she would say. "You just need to worry about a flight!" As much as I wanted to, I always found reason why I could not. I would often blame it on finances or the kids, but the real reason was much deeper than that. The real reason was my fear of the unknown and the messaging that I told myself that I was not someone who would ever be able to afford the luxury of travelling abroad.

As my personal development progressed and I started to reach higher levels of achievement in my work life I began to be exposed to different experiences. Before I knew it I was traveling all over the country and into the US for work. Travel started to become a norm for me. Instead of always saying no to new ideas and opportunities, I started to say yes. Every year Deb would continue to ask me to come visit her. Finally the time came that I said yes to her too! I told her that I was going to come and visit her that September. I think it was around May that I made that declaration. At first she didn't believe me. She would reach out to me weekly asking if I had booked my ticket. No after no she received until the day that I sent her my itinerary. She called me right away as she couldn't believe her eyes!

The day came for me to finally get on the plane. I had a short flight from Montreal to Toronto and then a redeye direct to Manchester. I was filled with anticipation and anxiety about spending so many hours in a plane flying over the ocean but I settled into my seat and I prepared for my long trip. Before I knew it the plane touched down in England and I was off to greet my childhood friend in the country she now called home. It was such an incredible feeling. Needless to say the trip with Deb was amazing. She was an incredibly host and traipsed me all over the country side. Together we enjoyed many wonderful sites and created amazing memories.

While I was in Europe I also took the opportunity to take a little side trip and spend four days in Rome. As this was a once in a life time trip for me, I decided that I would visit the city that had held me heart since I was a little girl while I had the chance. These four days were the most magical days of my life. I cried almost the entire time I was there. I am sure the locals must have thought I was crazy! I spent time at the Vatican exploring the museum, seeing the Pope, visiting the catacombs and of course experiencing the Sistine Chapel. To say it was magnificent is an understatement at best. As I sat in the chapel looking up at the Creation of Man tears streamed down my face. I could not believe that I was sharing the same space as the great Michelangelo. How incredibly blessed was I.

During my time in the amazing Roma I also visited the colosseum, the forum, the Spanish steps, the Cassola D' Angelo and of course the Trevi Fountain (where yes, I did make my wish). I also visited the most incredible churches and piazzas along the way. I shopped and I dined and I watched and I listened and I loved, loved, loved every second of my experience. An experience I would have never had if I had not gotten over my fears, pulled the trigger and took the action required to make it happen. One of the most interesting things I have learned about taking action with that trip is that once you do, it's not such a big deal any more.

Since my trip to England to visit my wonderful friend and my short stay in the incredible city of Rome I have opened myself up to even more travel and adventure. I have been to Frankfurt, Munich, Singapore, Venice, Verona, Florence, Naples, The Isle of Capri and of course back to my beloved Rome (this time with Deb meeting me there). I have also been all over Canada and the US. You see once I got over all the reasons that I told myself that I couldn't do it, it was no longer an impossible dream. My taking action altered my reality and changed my perspective from Europe being so far away to it being just another flight. Next on my list? Everywhere. So look out world! Here I come!!

Your Future:

So how can we initiate more action in our lives? Well first we need to recognize that like choice, action is already a part of everything we do. When you make your coffee in the morning you are taking action. When you get up to take the dog out for his morning relief, action. When you turn on the TV after planting your behind on the couch for the afternoon, yes that too is action. When you can start to see all the little ways in which you already take action throughout the day all of a sudden action does not sound like such a scary word. Once you understand this, perhaps taking some massive action will not be so far behind. To start however, let's see how we can implement so decisive action into our routine.

1. There is no time like the present.

There will never be a perfect time to take action. If you are waiting for the perfect time to get started it will never happen. You need to start now and make adjustments as you go. Trial and error will get you further than your non-start ever will.

2. Stop overthinking.

When you over analyze every single detail of every single thing you never ever get anything done. Yes there are a million ways to feed a cat, you just need to pick one and get on with it. If it turns out to be the wrong way, then you know better for next time.

3. Become a doer

Stop procrastinating and just do it. Stop tricking yourself into believing that you will do it after you finish the episode or play solitaire on your phone. We all know that you are just putting off the inevitable. Just go get it done so that you can bask in the glory of your accomplishment.

4. Face your fears

Whatever it is that is standing in the way of you and your dreams, get over it. You want to be a public speaker but you are afraid to talk in front of others? Do something about it. Take classes, join speaking clubs, do stand up. Once you realize that there is nothing to fear by fear itself, you are free to pursue all of your heart's desire. I mean really, what's the worse that can happen? You are judged or worse laughed at? No what is the worse is that you live to the end of your days never reaching your full potential

5. Say farewell to excuses

Do not waste another moment of your time on why you should not do something. Your time is much better spent focusing on why we should do something? Excuses are just a weak man's way out. There is an expression that goes, "If there is a will, there is a way!" Find your will and live like that!

6. Discard distractions

Take time and space to focus solely on what you are doing. Turn off the TV, close the door and put your phone on mute. Get rid of any and all things that are distracting to you and turn your attention entirely to the task at hand. Give yourself a set period of time and dedicate it to completely your task.

7. Reward yourself

Once you have completed whatever action you set out to accomplish, give yourself a little reward. Be it a congratulations, a check mark or something bigger like a coffee break or a treat. Whatever it is make sure you take some time to appreciate your victory. This will go a long way in your continuing to take action.

When it comes to taking massive action and reaching our goals, the rule of 5 is a great way to implement action into our days. Whether we dedicate 5 minutes, five actions or one action for five days. Deliberately setting aside time each day to move in the direction of your goals is more than most people do. If you can commit to taking action each day for 21 days you will not only be well on you way to achieving your goals but you will also be creating a habit that will help you to be more proactive in creating your future. So take action Jackson and you will sure to make your journey a triumphant one!

*"A playful path is the shortest
road to happiness."
~ Bernie DeKoven*

Chapter 11

PLANNING FOR PLAYFULNESS
The Finale

Congratulations! We have now reached the final chapter. I hope you have enjoyed reading this book as much as I have enjoyed writing it. I want you to know that in finishing this book you have done more for your wellbeing than many people do in a lifetime. Take a moment to recognize the time, energy and attention you put into implementing these 10 powerful concepts into your life. You should feel really good about what you have learned and where this learning will take you in your journey. My compliments on your commitment to self. It is now time to celebrate!

Of all the things that I have shared in this book I think the most important, yet often overlooked is the ability to play and have fun along our journey. As adults we get so caught up in the "realities" of life and fitting in all of the "must dos' that we forget to just enjoy. It is sad to think that we have been conditioned to believe that in order to be successful at adulting we must be serious and pious all the time. As I have learned throughout my journey, this just isn't so! Being playful is such an important part of being successful in life. Not only does it create greater joy for ourselves. Those of us who can remain playful are held in higher regard by others.

The reason I did not make playfulness a step is that I do not believe it is. To me being playful is not something that we need to deliberately implement into our lives, it should simply be a state of continuous being. I have learned that by having a little more childlike focus in our adult lives we become so much more proactive and productive. Let's face it every task is much more enjoyable when we can bring a playful attitude into its execution. The more fun we have in doing what needs to be done, the more we want to do it. Its simple logic really.

Besides, did you know that playfulness if one of the most attractive personality traits. The number one feature that is cited when women are asked what qualities they look for in a man is a sense of humour. Humour ranks in the top three traits for men too when asked what they are looking for in a mate. Makes sense as good dose of playfulness in a relationship can increase satisfaction between couples and as the playfulness grows, so does the relationship. I mean really, who doesn't want to have fun with their partner? As they say, couples who play together stay together.

Playful people are also much more successful in life. Studies have concluded that when you bring a playful attitude to your life, your level of achievement increases. Considering that people like to work with and buy from people that they like, this makes sense. When you have a lighter air to your presence, you generate more opportunities. Most people get so caught up in trying to impress others that they are not able to relax and just be themselves. When you can relax a little more and bring a little fun to your interactions, you are able to showcase more of your authentic self, which in turn develops deeper connections. I mean really, wouldn't you rather spend your time with someone who brings a little more sparkle into your world?

Speaking of sparkle, my father used to be the most serious man I ever knew. When I was a young girl I had the impression that my father was a man not to be messed with. He was the last person that we wanted to be in trouble with. All he had to do is use what came to be known as his poppa frown and we all knew we were in for it deep. There was no messing around with my dad. The boom of his voice when he told us to knock it off was enough to scare any kid straight. Nope, you did not want to be on the wrong side of my dad! Truth be told, for years I was afraid of my father.

After my parents' divorce however, I got to know a different side of him. Little by little my father started to reveal to me, what a big kid he was. How much fun he could have doing the simplest of things and how terribly immature his sense of humour was. I remember a time when I was about sixteen years old that I had gone to visit him. The small town that he lived in had awful radio reception and as a tormented teenager, music was my life As soon as I walked into his house I would head directly to the tv, unplug the cable and hook it up to the stereo so that I could listen to my favourite FM station. Dad never stopped me. He knew I needed it. One day however, as I was sitting in the livingroom listen to my beloved tunes, my father started to strut into the room, belly out, back swayed walking pigeoned toed and with a massive swagger proclaimed "Disco Daddy is in the house!" I could not believe what I was seeing. We both broke into laugher. That memory has never ever faded from me.

Over the years I learned how silly my father really was. I can share countless stories of the fun that we used to have together. I recall all the ways in which he would play with his grandchildren, tease his wife and have a joke ready for anyone and everyone who was in his vicinity. He was such a funny guy and of course, I wanted to be just like him, so I became his sidekick. We used to watch cartoons, play card games, read stupid magazines and laugh at Calvin & Hobbs comics together. Of course my favourite pastime of ours was trying to outdo one another in our attempts to get a rise out of other family members. Yes, my father and I made quite a hilarious team. As the years passed, there was hardly a time when my father didn't meet me with a sparkle in his eye.

When I look back at who he thought he had to be when I was a child vs who he showed me he was when I was a young adult, I realized that we can get so lost in being an adult sometimes. As a young father my dad thought that he had to be serious to be effective. Over the years he realized that in order to be effective, he had to be authentic. My dad taught me that you can be responsible AND still have fun. The two do not have to be mutually exclusive. As a matter of fact, I believe that the more fun you have, the more responsible you become. For when you are enjoying your life, you want to step up and make sure that you don't do anything to jeopardize it!

Not only that, but studies have shown that people who have a more playful approach to life are more creative in their problem solving abilities. Most complex problems that adults face in both their personal and professional lives require creative solutions. Being playful not only helps to jump start the creative process, it can break us out of our cognizant habits that are holding us back in so many areas of our lives. Playing helps us to shape our brain and aids us in coming across situations we have never experienced before and learn from them. Consider that when children are young they are uninhibited and unselfconscious in their play. Without hesitation, they are constantly seeking our new experiences to engage their minds and imaginations. They take in everything around them with curiosity and intrigue just like little sponges. This is what makes them such quick and insatiable learners. By adopting this attitude of play as adults, we are provided with the same potential to become smarter as well.

For years I have said that I would like to build a retreat for adults filled with the activities of our youth. A place where we would go to play like we once did as children. There would be a finger painting center, a mud pie kitchen, bike riding trails, a tree climbing apparatus (accompanied with crash pads of course), fort building, basketball hoops, games centers and playgrounds filled with monkey bars, swing sets and teeter totters. Each day would consist of three different activities with an hour or two of open play. Meals would consist of peanut butter and jelly sandwiches, home make mac n' cheese and hotdogs. All veggies will be ground up and hidden in our smoothies and desserts (like carrot cake). And the piece de resistance of course would be that each night we would end with a good old game of hide and seek.

Can you imagine how great this could be? Just thinking about this concept has elevated your emotional state you have to admit (Who knows, maybe this vision will become a reality one day). As adults we stop doing the things that we did as children that assisted in our development. Even when it comes to meeting new people. As children we would find ourselves standing before some new kid staring blankly at one another until one of us asks, "Do you like riding bikes?" (or whatever the activity is) and when the answer is yes we run off together and a friendship is formed. As adults we stand around like idiots, afraid to talk to one another for fear of being judged or worse rejected. So unless we have ingested some sort of liquid courage, or are forced to communicate by some other means, we just keep to ourselves.

We don't engage, we don't adopt new interactions and we don't put ourselves out of our comfort zone. As kids, we never remained in our comfort zone. We were always expanding, exploring and learning. Today it is even worse with the invention of products such as the smart phone. We can now communicate without ever being in another person's presence. We hide behind fake personas and live more distant from one another than ever. In this disconnect we forget what it is like to be authentic and to create bonds with others. We live in a society that is feeling more and more isolated and alone. The increase of mental illness and suicide is on the rise. As the world folds in on us and our focus becomes more honed in on ourselves, we create an environment full of pain. Internally and externally. This is not how we were designed to live. Life was meant to be lived in a community and it was meant to be enjoyed. We are struggling because we no longer feel congruent with who we are designed to be.

Each of us as individuals have a responsibility to live an authentic life that is consistent with who we have the potential to be. When we live small we not only sell ourselves short, but the entire world. We may feel that we are alone in the world, but we are all connected and we have a responsibility to one another. As we awake as individuals we help the global conscientiousness awake a whole. We think that we are but one small particle and have no impact on making any great change. This is not true, as individuals, we are the only ones that have any impact at all. Like the drop of water in the ocean, it may seem inconsequential on the whole, but the whole is made up of a multitude of single drops.

Now before you have a panic attack and think this is just far too much responsibility. Let me bring it back down for you. Our responsibility to the world is to show up in our most progressive manner each and every day. The reason I chose the word progressive is that we are all continuously on our journey of growth whether we are aware of it or not. So if we approach each day conscientiously committed to being our best version of self for that one day only, we will make a huge impact on all of those that we interact with as we move through our lives. By simply being the best version of you, you never know who you will impact or in what way you many change another's life. I am always awed and humbled when someone around me shares that I have inspired them in one way or another.

So go out into your world as children. Laugh, dance, play and love. Find all the reasons to celebrate. Focus on what is good. Share your passion and dreams with others. Don't take life so seriously and definitely don't take yourself so seriously. Do not be afraid to fail. Just in trying alone you are far ahead of the pack. Lead where you need to lead, follow when you need to follow. Trust in yourself, in others and in the universe. Know how special you are and how much you matter. Never fear being judged or rejected. You are perfect in your own unique and wonderful way. The world needs what you have to offer. Live authentic and when others meet you with resistance know that it is about them and not you. Offer them love and then keep going. Go and grow and grow and grow! You've got this!!

One of the greatest gifts my father ever gave me was to be able to witness him as he become more and more playful as he aged. He taught me that laughing every day is not only super healthy but it also keeps things in perspective. Life is meant to be enjoyed. The more occasion we take to enjoy all of the merriment that life offers, the more merriment we have to enjoy. As I always say, *"I am very serious about life, but I don't take life very seriously"*.

In peace and in love...

Stephanie

ABOUT THE AUTHOR

Stephanie is a Canadian writer, blogger and all round artist and creative being. Working as a freelance writer and marketing writer, Stephanie has written professionally for over 10 years. Not only has she penned and published many technical articles and newspaper reports but has also written the Zen Matter Workbook series. She is currently working on two additional manuscripts and runs a blog. As a professional working in the corporate world she combines her logical brain with her emotional heart, sharing the insights she has learned along the way that has helped her to live a life filled with love, abundance and success.

Stephanie dubs herself a "Creative Extraordinaire" and revels in her understanding of how we are all the masters of our own universe and have the ability to create the world we want to live in. They joy she takes from observing her own reality unfold in unimaginable ways inspires her to help others to achieve the same. She strongly believes in the philosophy of "Reach one. Teach one" and claims that any and all success is achieved by cultivating the right mindset. For it does not matter where you begin, but only where you chose to end!

Manufactured by Amazon.ca
Bolton, ON

33535167R00085